CHEF

2022

"Chef Ricky's recipes are secular and sacred. They exist between the soul of a Friday night fish fry and the gospel of a Sunday afternoon fish stew. *Saltbox Seafood Joint Cookbook* captures the rhythm where the Neuse and Trent Rivers meet with recipes that call for extended dinner tables and multiple second helpings."
—**SHIRLETTE AMMONS**, writer, producer, and musician whose albums include *Language Barrier* and *Spectacles*

"Ricky Moore should be named a STATE TREASURE for his indescribably delicious work and passion that allows us to savor the distinctive seafood of North Carolina and the coastal South. Here he teaches us that good fish—anywhere—is local, seasonal, fresh, and simply prepared."
—**MARCIE COHEN FERRIS**, author of *The Edible South*

"A cookbook that puts seafood up front, demystifying the process of selecting, prepping, and then frying, broiling, and grilling to perfection. Ricky Moore traces his evolution from the New Bern fishing hole to his military service, culinary school training, and experiences working as a chef at top restaurants—and then he recounts the wonderful story of how he started his restaurants in Durham, North Carolina. And I really savored the explanation behind his Hush-Honeys."
—**BRIDGETTE A. LACY**, author of *Sunday Dinner: A Savor the South Cookbook*

"*Saltbox Seafood Joint Cookbook* is a treasure that will be savored and read cover to cover by seafood lovers. Ricky Moore has focused his eye, from childhood to the present, on fish—catching, cooking, and eating it. His mantra is simplicity, breathtaking simplicity, and doing one thing well. He is the acknowledged master of cooking seafood."
—**WILLIAM FERRIS**, author of *The South in Color: A Visual Journal*

Saltbox Seafood Joint® Cookbook

Seasonal Seafood Freshly Cooked,

Good Fish That's the Hook®

SALTBOX SEAFOOD JOINT

— EST. 2012 —

COOKBOOK

Ricky Moore

Written with K. C. Hysmith

THE UNIVERSITY OF NORTH CAROLINA PRESS   CHAPEL HILL

This book was published with the assistance of the Blythe Family Fund

of the University of North Carolina Press.

Manufactured in the United States of America

Designed by Kimberly Bryant and set in Whitman by Rebecca Evans

The University of North Carolina Press has been a member of the Green Press Initiative

since 2003.

Cover photograph courtesy of Briana Brough.

Library of Congress Cataloging-in-Publication Data

Names: Moore, Ricky, author. | Hysmith, K. C. (Katherine C.)

Title: Saltbox Seafood Joint cookbook / Ricky Moore; written with K. C. Hysmith.

Description: Chapel Hill : The University of North Carolina Press, [2019] |

Includes index.

Identifiers: LCCN 2019011821| ISBN 9781469653532 (cloth : alk. paper) |

ISBN 9781469653549 (ebook)

Subjects: LCSH: Saltbox Seafood Joint. | Cooking (Seafood)—North Carolina. |

LCGFT: Cookbooks.

Classification: LCC TX747 .M774 2019 | DDC 641.6/92—dc23

LC record available at https://lccn.loc.gov/2019011821

To my wife, Norma, for asking the question, "Where can I get a
good fish sandwich?" and for all her wonderful support over the years.
Being the spouse of a chef takes a special kind of person.

.....

Big shout out, high-five, and salute to my daughter, Hunter Johanna,
and my son, Greyson Beckham, for always being my inspiration.

.....

And, finally, to all the hardworking fishermen, crabbers, and oystermen
in North Carolina; without them, Saltbox Seafood Joint would not be.

CONTENTS

Acknowledgments **ix**

INTRODUCTION The Story of Saltbox Seafood **1**

THE FISH KITCHEN RULES

School Lessons: Fish Varieties **18**

Knife Work: Cuts **25**

What's Running When: Seasonality **27**

Helpful Kitchen Equipment **28**

Sources for Fish and Know-How **28**

STANDARD OPERATING PROCEDURE Stocks, Seasonings, and Sauces **29**

FRIED AND JOY Pan-Frying and Deep-Frying **41**

INTO THE COALS Grilling, Smoking, and Charcoaling **59**

ONE-POTS Soups, Chowders, and Stews **75**

PERFECT HOMINY Grits and Seafood **97**

THE SPREAD Hot and Cold Sides **113**

MENUS **130**

Line Drawing Credits **132**

Index **133**

SIDEBARS

Fish Grease versus Other Grease **40**

Freeman's Beach / Seabreeze **46**

Definition—"Calabash" **48**

Definition—"Fried Hard" **54**

A Bake Is Really a Boil **62**

Smoked Fish **69**

Please Don't Say Trashfish/Uglyfish **82**

White Bread Bone Cushion **95**

Grits, Shrimp, Pork, and Gravy **100**

No Such Thing as North Carolina Dinner Grits **110**

West Indies Salad Mythology **116**

Church Spreads and Cucumber and Onion Salad **127**

ACKNOWLEDGMENTS

With gratitude, I would like to thank everyone who has supported the start-up and growth of a little 205-square-foot space located on Mangum Street in the Old Five Points neighborhood in Durham.

Special thanks to Dock to Door, Locals Seafood, Murray L. Nixon Fishery, Salty Catch Seafood, and Washington Crab & Oyster Company. Thanks also to NC Catch, the North Carolina Fisheries Association, and the Core Sound Waterfowl Museum & Heritage Center.

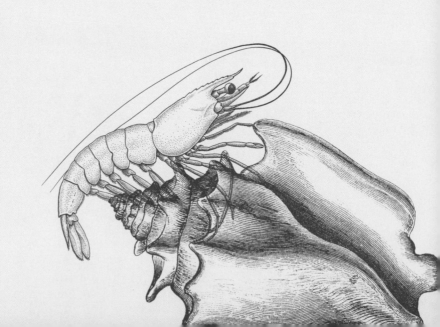

Saltbox Seafood Joint® Cookbook

Chef Ricky seasoning his Country Fried Potatoes with Onions and Green Peppers. Author's collection.

The Story of Saltbox Seafood

Growing Up in New Bern

Local seafood is my gospel and always has been. My mother's side of the family came from a community called Riverdale, situated between New Bern and Havelock. My father was from Harlowe, halfway between Beaufort and New Bern. You crossed waters whichever way you went. I grew up along the Neuse and Trent Rivers and spent plenty of my childhood fishing those waters, but I don't want this to sound as though we were eating fish all the time. We ate it whenever we could get it, whenever it was available, or whenever somebody went out fishing. This was real life, so we ate standard eastern North Carolina stuff, too, like greens with white cornmeal dumplings and salted pig tails, collard sandwiches, tender flat biscuits, fried chicken, and iceberg lettuce covered with thick salad dressing. It was never all fish.

A lot of people in my area didn't have traditional families or upbringings where the mother or grandmother stayed home and cooked everything from scratch. They had jobs, too. My mother worked at the local hospital for a long time. She was incredibly busy, but when she had time to cook she always did it in a very organized way. At no point in her process was the kitchen ever a mess—she kept things clean and neat, and made things like "priddy fried chicken," clean fried fish, and meatloaf with a tight and tidy ketchup glaze on top. My maternal grandmother, Bernice, worked in a Havelock school cafeteria and would bring home all sorts of extras from work. Hot, scratch-made dishes like lasagna,

Elementary school days. Author's collection.

chicken tetrazzini, yeast rolls, and hamburger steak and gravy. Bernice had a close companion named James—we called him Tick—who learned to cook when he was stationed at Cherry Point. He was a kind of grandfather figure to me (and later married my grandmother Bernice) and was always cooking good food. Tick was known for his big breakfasts. They weren't anything fancy—standard eggs and potatoes, fresh sausage, boiled and pan-fried ham, and bacon with a thick rind on it—but they were always done with precision.

Food and work were always tied up together. In the summertime, when we wanted some pocket money, all of us kids would get on our bikes and ride across the Bridgeton Bridge to go pick blueberries at Morris Blueberry Farm. The earlier you got there the sooner you could finish before it got too hot. The farm paid in crisp, clean dollars that stuck together when you first got them.

My first official job was in a barbershop where I ran errands, shined shoes, and swept up the hair from the floor. My aunt got me the job. Down the street from the shop, a lady would cook food and sell plates heaped high with fried chicken, roast beef, chitlins, barbecue ribs, macaroni and cheese, collards, corn pudding, and such. I took orders, ran to collect the plates, and brought them back to the barbershop. At the end of the day, I spent the tips on a plate just for myself. Later, I ran a paper route, but I spent all my money on candy, so my mother made me quit. In high school, I worked at the Piggly Wiggly as a bagger, cashier, and produce stocker. Then I took another job as a dishwasher at a local seafood restaurant called Friday's 1890. They never made the kind of fish you ate at home; instead, they made popcorn shrimp, fried flounder, hushpuppies, all the normal sides, and classic North Carolina pulled pork barbecue. A lot of restaurants did pork and seafood, like an eastern North Carolina surf and turf, and served it all on the same plate. I've always wondered why barbecue took the lead.

Life was busy, and everybody had work to do, so we didn't always gather at the table together to eat, but the food we had was always nurturing. Whatever I was fed, whichever friend or family made it, it was good to me. And, thankfully, we still found time for fishing.

During the summer all the cousins would gather at my other grandmother Lottie Mae's house. Once a week or so we'd set off on very informal fishing excursions with bamboo fishing poles fitted with standard bits of bait. Whenever you did go fishing, everybody caught enough for everybody—at least, that was the plan anyways. We'd haul our catch home for our aunts and grandmother to do the extra-messy job of scaling, gutting, and cleaning (they never trusted us kids to do it). When we couldn't make it out to the water, there was a gentleman who drove around selling freshly caught fish in his pickup truck that he had outfitted with a wood and galvanized tin storage setup and a big metal scale. All the fish was stored on ice—it seemed so special. You made your selection and he would weigh it out and wrap it up for you to take back into the house. Fish was either fried or stewed, depending on the size of the catch, and always very simply prepared. It was served with boiled potatoes or other some vegetable. Everybody, even us kids, ate the same thing.

Military Life

After graduating high school, I thought I would go to East Carolina University and learn to be an artist. I had good eye for mimicking life and a talent for drawing and painting, but I also knew that I didn't have the discipline for school right then. I liked working and earning a paycheck and hoped to travel.

Before we settled in New Bern, I had been an army brat. I was born on the base at Cherry Point, but we quickly moved to Schweinfurt, Germany, where my dad was stationed. He was a sergeant first class and worked with the artillery. My mother stayed home and cooked very American meals with the very American ingredients we could source on base, but I had a German babysitter who fed me pints of local raspberries picked that day and freshly baked bread that she slathered with butter. I still remember the smell. And I remember hot roast

chicken and pommes frites with mayonnaise, too. There I was, a little kid with an afro and an orange Fat Albert shirt, soaking up all the German food culture, and I was hooked.

I knew the military could give me these kinds of adventures again, so in 1987, I enlisted as soon as I turned eighteen. I completed basic training and went to jump school at Fort Benning, Georgia, to learn to be a paratrooper. When it came time to choose my AIT (Advanced Initial Training), I picked the first option that would get me out of New Bern: military cook school in Fort Jackson, South Carolina!

Just like any other part of the military, cook school was full of procedure. I learned army food regulations, military facilities operations, and combat field feeding. Contrary to popular belief, the food served in the military isn't slop. We quickly learned that meals had to sustain, had to be wholesome, and had to feed a lot of people. There was a regulation for everything. There were military recipes, and the recipes were our regulations. There was even a recipe for Kool-Aid. All the recipes were filed in a color-coded index: yellow for poultry, orange for meat, green for vegetables, and blue for seafood. All were designed to be scaled in order to feed twenty-five, fifty, seventy-five, or even a hundred people at a time. I learned a lot from these regulations: how to read a recipe, how to scale a recipe for a crowd, how to measure, and how to cook in huge vessels and vats. Every military kitchen is headed by a senior food service sergeant, which translates in civilian terms to an executive chef. Each role has a counterpart in the classical French kitchen.

As I traveled to each new station, from Fort Polk, Louisiana, to the Schofield Barracks in Hawaii, I learned new regulations and new styles of food particular to that region or state. Along the way, I met my future wife, Norma, who was

On graduating from the Culinary Institute of America, 1994. Author's collection.

also stationed in Hawaii. We were married in four months. When we were ready to leave Hawaii, my chief warrant officer persuaded me to pursue culinary school. He told me about the Culinary Institute of America (CIA) and how it had been founded by veterans returning from the war. The CIA was the next logical place for me to go.

Norma was still enlisted and soon stationed at Fort Huachuca, Arizona. I got a civilian job working in a dining facility on the base. I quickly rose to become a manager and found myself even more ready for culinary school. As soon as we could, we packed up the car and drove to upstate New York to start my next round of training.

Culinary School and Starting a Career

In 1993, I enrolled in a two-year program at the CIA and Norma started a program nearby at SUNY–New Paltz. New York State had generous veterans' benefits, so we could both focus on school. I spent a lot of time in the CIA library, especially during the cold winter months. I had eaten well all my life and I had cooked food, but there was still so much to learn. Along the way I kept finding connections, threads that tied my experiences together. The famed French chef Auguste Escoffier created the kitchen brigade system, La Brigade, which organized a system of command in the kitchen. I remember thinking, "This is exactly what we have in the military." The structure felt organic and natural. My basic training as a soldier wasn't so different from learning kitchen fundamentals, but in culinary school you get the bonus of learning about wine pairings and the practical economics of running a restaurant kitchen. I staged (the culinary school term for interning) in wonderful kitchens like Daniel in

Manhattan and the old-school Westchester Country Club in Rye, New York. I went where I needed to in order to learn as much as I could. My goal was to be a great chef, period.

After we both graduated, Norma and I moved to Washington, D.C., to be closer to her family and to start my career in the culinary world. My first job was at a hot little Italian restaurant called Galileo. Over the next decade, I hopped from one exciting kitchen to another, working with all kinds of cuisines, including upscale southern at Vidalia, global French at Lespinasse, country provincial at Provence, regional mid-Atlantic at Equinox, and French-inflected Lebanese at Le Tarbouche. I eventually became executive chef at Le Relais, a new restaurant with a focus on dishes from the French countryside. To help construct the menu, the owners took me to Paris, where I staged in traditional kitchens.

It was part of my personal practice to further my culinary education and experience by working abroad whenever I had the opportunity. I wanted to work in specific restaurants just to define for myself what, exactly, a Michelin-starred kitchen was and what made it so special. Through this work abroad, I found a shared sense of tradition, culture, behavior, and, most important, discipline when it came to food and dining.

I was the only person of color in these European kitchens, which made me even more intense about learning as much as possible. Back then, the only African American chef I knew of was Patrick Clark, who ran famous restaurants like Odeon and Tavern on the Green and was on *Iron Chef* back before the show was big in the United States. Being black automatically pigeonholed you. By focusing on the classical cuisines of France and Italy, Clark was never perceived as a typical African American chef. Not wanting to be recognized as just a southern cook, I thought that I should follow a similar path.

After some time and additional stages in European restaurants, I realized that the rustic roots of these culinary mainstays weren't that different from the food of my childhood. I began to see that southern food is not a lesser cuisine, and I shed many of the insecurities I had held about my own food culture. It was time to head back to the States.

We landed in Chicago, where I worked with Charlie Trotter for a couple

Chef Ricky at "A Taste of Heritage" event at the Hay Adams Hotel in Washington, D.C., around 1995. Chef Edna Lewis is standing in the back row, second from left, and chef Patrick Clark is next to her, third from left. Ricky is in the front row, fourth from left. Author's collection.

of weeks. He introduced me to some other folks, and I found myself working with Oprah and her chef, Art Smith, to promote his new cookbook. I worked in another stage at Frontera Grill with Rick Bayless before assuming the executive chef position at Southwater Kitchen, a restaurant that specialized in contemporary home cooking, a kind of elevated American midwestern cuisine. Shortly after, I left to help open the revamped Washburne Culinary Institute with one of my former CIA instructors, William Reynolds. While there, I served as the chef instructor of the culinary school restaurant, the Parrot Cage.

From there Norma and I headed back to D.C., where I became executive chef at Agraria (now known as Founding Farmers). I happily settled back into the D.C. bustle and was soon recruited to do an episode of *Iron Chef* against the newly jacketed Michael Symon, who later became one of the hosts of ABC's *The Chew*, for his very first battle. I had watched this show religiously and still couldn't believe that my field was a competitive sport. Our battle theme was "Thanksgiving" and Symon won (though I think he shouldn't have). Life in Washington kept us busy, and our family was growing; it was time to move again. This time we headed back to North Carolina, settling in Chapel Hill with my goal of opening a business for myself. I knew it was time.

Singapore to Saltbox

One day Norma asked me where she could get a good fried fish sandwich (she grew up in a fisherman family, too). I realized that I didn't have an answer for her. She wanted a sandwich made with local fish, lightly breaded and seasoned, fried in fresh oil until golden brown and delicious, then served on fresh slices of yeasty sweet bread and garnished with traditional cooked green pepper and spicy onion relish plus tartar sauce chock full of capers, cornichons, eggs, and herbs. No local seafood restaurant had what she wanted, but I knew I could make that sandwich. That's when I realized I needed a place to do something for myself. I started to explore different Durham neighborhoods. Although I didn't have an exact idea of what I was looking for, I knew that if I saw the right space, I could plug something in. I remembered growing up and going to little places that did one thing only but did it really well.

These little places appeared again in my life during my travels in Asia. Singapore, for example, is known for its open-air hawkers' markets—the widely known "wet markets"—with food halls and one-person shops that do one thing really well. Amid the hustle and bustle of the streets, the smoke and lights and tricycles loaded high with random stuff, there are little side shops with outside seating and simple menus. One shop I remember made the unofficial national dish of Singapore: traditional chili crabs with a sauce spiked with American ketchup and lots of black pepper. The chef had everything in its place and a spice box filled with ground chilis and black pepper. With all the pepper, you might think that chili crabs are really spicy, but they are perfectly balanced. Shellfish need spice, be it black pepper or Old Bay Seasoning. After you ordered, the chef took these abnormally large Sri Lankan crabs, steamed them gently over greens in a wok, and stopped them halfway to finish them with a sweet and spicy glaze. Customers trickled in all night long looking for a quick bite and a beer. The chef continued at his wok, adding crabs and chili peppers to keep up with the flow.

Ricky standing in front of the original Saltbox Seafood Joint on North Mangum Street in Durham. Photograph by Baxter Miller, used by permission.

The original Saltbox Seafood Joint on North Mangum Street in Durham. Photograph by Baxter Miller, used by permission.

The Saltbox Seafood Joint catering truck.
Photograph by Baxter Miller, used by permission.

To Do One Thing Really Well

I wanted a little shop, to do one thing really well, and to control every aspect of it. This was ultimately the base of my business model. Singapore stayed in the back of my mind during my search and was my first thought when I finally found a small building, a little walkup with the right bones, that wouldn't require a lot of staff and would allow me to be in a place where I was there every day doing it all myself. A place where I wanted to be all the time. Seafood just made sense.

Unfortunately, this little shop was not for rent and was occupied by a burger and hot dog joint, so I decided to observe this operation's routine. For about a week, I went there in the morning, at noontime, and late at night. I observed the traffic patterns, the local activities, the types of customers on foot and in cars, and the neighborhood vibe. I also watched the business. The owners weren't working the place as I thought they should have been. They were always late, glued to the loud television in the restaurant kitchen, and seemed to have no interest in serving food. So, I thought I would ask them, "You must be tired of this?" They were a little offended.

I talked to the building's owner, an elderly lady whose family had owned the place for a long time, and I told her about what I wanted to do and what the place could be. Thankfully, the timing was right, the old business left, we drew up a new lease, and I found myself with a small restaurant without bells and whistles and in need of a thorough cleaning and complete reorganization.

Then came the naysayers. "You going to go to that little building over there?" "We've seen so many different things in there. . . ." "You're coming in here with seafood, okay, . . . you'll be gone in three months." But they were all missing the boat. I had driven around this neighborhood and seen firsthand the changes that were coming. I knew, five years from now, this would be a success—I could get it done. This was a practical opportunity to go into business for myself, do something creative and thoughtful, without big loans or investors. I could work this little thing.

Soon the questions changed. "Where did you find this space? It's so cool!" Seeing the success, the people who ran the burger stand before me even came back and wanted to take over my lease. People were really excited about what I was doing, and it seemed as if every chef in Durham came by to eat. As a chef, I feel that I know what chefs like: goodness, simple goodness, and to taste the care in what we're eating.

My original plan was to have a food truck (it was all the rage at the time). Instead, I got a stationary concession stand with two small fryers and a four-burner range. I was cooking everything to order. And I found I could do everything I wanted all for myself. I had Saltbox.

For me, Saltbox means hometown, and I kept this in mind as I created the menu. I wanted to bring that hometown food forward. I did my research and asked, "What was your hometown food in Durham?" The default answer was always pulled pork. Growing up in New Bern, it was fried hard crabs or fried

Ricky on a boat headed for Cedar Island
Core Sound for clam digging. Photograph by
Baxter Miller, used by permission.

Ricky with his wife, Norma Moore,
in Cape Hatteras on the North Carolina
Outer Banks, 2017. Author's collection.

chicken from Melvin's Chicken Shack, where they cooked chicken to order and you'd wait a while but never complain. In Chapel Hill there was the Rathskeller, where you could get the best spaghetti dinner, and Hector's, which was known far and wide for its wraps before wraps were cool. I wanted Saltbox to be a place like this, a place folks would consider part of their hometown and the fabric of the community. A place that would make folks say, "You ain't been to Durham if you haven't been to Saltbox." I opened the doors in October 2012, just in time for the first fish running of the fall.

Four years on, after staying steady, preaching the gospel about local seafood, and having confidence in my work, I decided to expand. As I drove back and forth between my home in Chapel Hill and my work in Durham, I kept passing the old Shrimp Boat restaurant. I thought, "If this space ever comes available, it would be ideal for a sit-down Saltbox." Through word of mouth, I found out that the Shrimp Boat's owners wanted to leave, so I jumped. Norma and I went through the bank process, cleaned up the space together, and turned the restaurant into a seamless second version of Saltbox. We painted the bricks the signature Saltbox colors that always remind me of the beach: the light green of seagrass, the orange of life preservers and fishermen's jumpsuits, and a light blue to represent North Carolina. Everything needed to be authentic. For inspiration, I visited the Core Sound Waterfowl Museum on Harkers Island, noting all the natural wood and the purposeful lack of mermaids, pirates, and anchors. Locals Seafood sent over cleaned oyster shells that we spread under the picnic tables situated beneath our giant vintage 1969 marquee. The marquee is how I communicate with my customers, building a space of awareness about local seafood and letting folks know what fish is in season. Although I use social media, I like this old-fashioned version, too. I'll spell out "Croaker Season" or "Butterfish is here" and watch as the cars pull in with curiosity. As a final touch, two vintage boat clocks hang over the door, so both customers and cooks can see the time and understand the importance of how this process of slow, local food works.

Culinary Philosophy: The Freshest Fish, Locally Sourced

My philosophy for Saltbox is the same as my general approach to food: simplicity. The more complicated something is, the more work it is. For Saltbox, this means sourcing seafood locally and handwriting menus on chalkboard to adapt to seasonal changes and avoid printing costs. From the beginning, I have been intent on serving what I want to serve; new dishes are introduced in a way that is slow and easy.

This philosophy extends to how I have chosen suppliers, such as Amanda Wells Miller from Door to Dock and the folks over at Locals Seafood. In the beginning, there was a perception that I was driving down to the coast and catching my own fish. What I actually did was seek out fishermen who could bring the fish to me, which is how I found Ricky Nixon from Murray L. Nixon Fishery in Edenton and fourth-generation fisherman Steve Goodwin from Salty Catch. At Locals Seafood, Lin Peterson and Ryan Speckman have mastered the fish-processing component, a skill that I would have to teach my cooks and just don't have time to do. They are quick to tell you that they aren't fishermen, but they have been passionate about understanding and educating themselves about their market, their people, their brand, and what they can promise. My mission has been to source seafood strictly from North Carolina fishermen. Saltbox would never have been successful if Locals Seafood had not been doing the great things they do for native fish and North Carolina seafood.

Thanks to these suppliers, I have my choice of local fish varieties, but I began my menus using fish that people could identify. At first I served the usual suspects, such as trout and flounder. Soon I expanded to less familiar species like bluefish, mullet, and Spanish mackerel. Cooking fresh, local seafood was my priority, but I quickly realized that I had to educate my customers, too. I graded the fish along a spectrum of oiliness: trout in the middle, full flavored to the right, and mild to the left. I'd tell folks, "You like trout? Well, you'll like mullet." Trout was a reference point that people seemed to like, and after they came and tasted the quality of the fish, they'd quickly accept more recommendations.

There was an unlisted Trust-Me Menu, made up of fish varieties that most people wouldn't normally eat. I'd give them a small portion for free, hoping to

Ricky with Steven Goodwin, fisherman, friend, and one of the key suppliers of the daily catch to Saltbox Seafood Joint. Photograph by Baxter Miller, used by permission.

Ricky cooking Stewed Clams and Country Sausage. Photograph by Baxter Miller, used by permission.

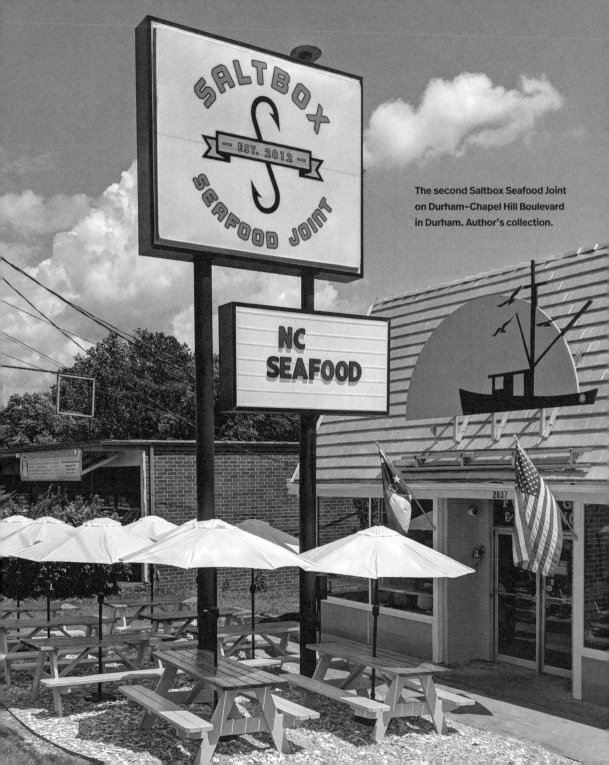

The second Saltbox Seafood Joint on Durham–Chapel Hill Boulevard in Durham. Author's collection.

earn their trust. I would say, "I'm not going to serve you something bad." Soon people felt as if I was spoiling them. They would sit and wait in line for hours because they knew I was doing things right and doing it just for them. They started to care about fish and put their trust and faith in me.

That's about when people started writing articles, focusing on all the good cooking and thankfully overlooking the downsides (such as that we didn't have a dining room or that there was always a line). Saltbox quickly became a platform for me to advocate for good cooking, evangelize local North Carolina seafood, and give back to the community. It's important to give back and give back genuinely, not just because you're supposed to, but because you are connected to it all. I've had the great fortune to partner with many meaningful events from fundraising dinners for homeless organizations to working with Durham Independent School District kitchen managers to create recipes for school cafeteria menus. Recent events I have held with Adrian Lindsay and the Green Book Supper Club, a pop-up dinner series showcasing African American chefs in North Carolina, have even inspired much of the historic and cultural research for this cookbook. The Green Book was an annual guidebook for African Americans during the Jim Crow era that pointed out shops, hotels, and restaurants that were friendly to the black community. Back then there were two places in Durham where you could stop and grab a bite to eat. Ultimately these places were a way to bring folks together. Change seems to happen if you put good food in front of people.

The Fish Kitchen Rules

School Lessons: Fish Varieties

When you go to the market or fishmonger, take time to verify the selection of seafood. If you're not sure about a particular variety or offering, just ask. Here's what I do: pay attention to visual cues (for example, bright clear eyes, crimson-red gills, shiny and firm flesh), note the aroma in the space, and ask the monger to present you the fish for a closer inspection. With the help of your local seafood expert, you will learn the various varieties of fish and better understand which specific native species work in the recipes you want to cook.

INCLUDES »

croaker

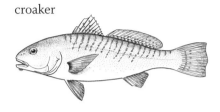

hogfish (pigfish)

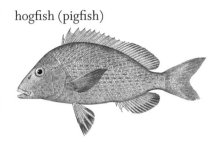

spot

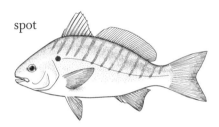

sugar toad

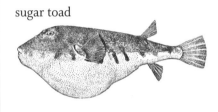

white/yellow perch

sea mullet (whiting)

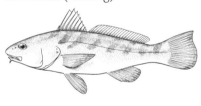

VARIETY » Round fish

DESCRIPTION » Refers to the roundness of the fillets

INCLUDES »

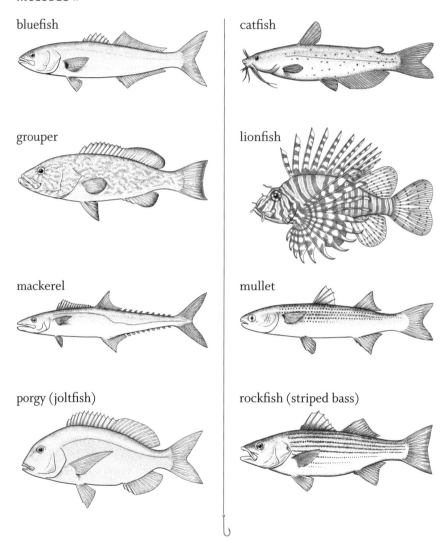

bluefish

catfish

grouper

lionfish

mackerel

mullet

porgy (joltfish)

rockfish (striped bass)

sheepshead

snapper

tripletail

trout (speckled trout)

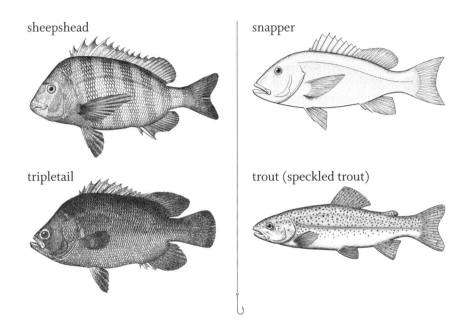

VARIETY » Flatfish

DESCRIPTION » Adult species swim horizontally

INCLUDES »

butterfish (harvestfish)

flounder

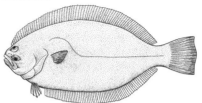

ribbonfish

VARIETY » Shellfish

DESCRIPTION » Varieties with shell or shell-like exteriors

INCLUDES »

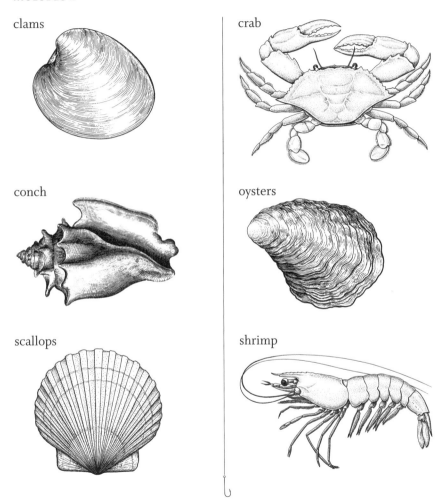

clams

crab

conch

oysters

scallops

shrimp

VARIETY » Loin fish

DESCRIPTION » Varieties that are typically sold in steaks or by whole loins

INCLUDES »

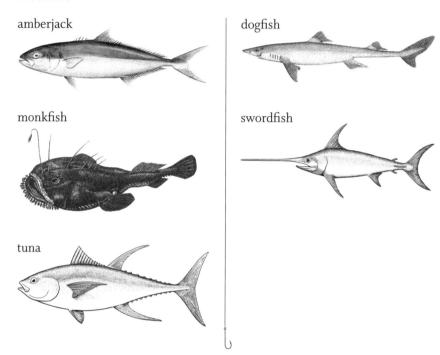

amberjack

dogfish

monkfish

swordfish

tuna

Knife Work: Cuts

As a kid, we knew to haul our catch home, so the grownups could properly clean and cut it for cooking. My folks would scale fish with an old butcher knife that they sharpened on a brick. Cleaning fish always seemed like such a chore, but I later learned the importance of cleaning and cutting fish correctly. Understanding specific cuts of fish is just as important as understanding the fish varieties. Whether you're cleaning your own catch or placing an order at the local fish market, you want to get the most for your time and money. Folks are likely familiar with many of these cuts, but a few are traditional to eastern North Carolina. Butterflied fish, for example, is a very Down East thing. Fish prepared this way look bigger, fry up crisp, and are easy to eat.

CUT	DESCRIPTION	VARIETY TYPICALLY FROM
fillet	a long, thin cutlet	flounder, catfish, mullet, mackerel
whole	a whole fish with head intact or removed, unscaled and ungutted	snapper, flounder, croaker, spot, butterfish (harvestfish)
steak	a thick cut typically sourced from a loin of denser fish; these cuts are firm to the touch, not flaky, and, well, steaklike	swordfish, tuna, dogfish
butterflied	a whole fish splayed open in two and easy to fry in a pan; ask for this special cut from your seafood provider or do it yourself	any whole pan fish that can be dressed

CUT	DESCRIPTION	VARIETY TYPICALLY FROM
collar	a cut sourced from the flesh from around the throat	amberjack, grouper, swordfish
dressed	guts are out; also referred to as scaled and gutted (s&g) and scaled and gutted and fins removed (s&g&f)	all nonloin fish can be dressed
shelled	crustaceans that are peeled or cracked open with their exoskeletons removed	shrimp and crab
shucked	shellfish that have been completely removed from their shell	clams, oysters, scallops, mussels, mollusks, conch. *Note*: When buying shellfish in the shell, look for tightly closed shells; an open shell indicates that the creature is dead and will have started to decompose

What's Running When: Seasonality

Just as crops have different growing seasons, so fish availability and variety change with the seasons. Fish, or at least one kind of fish, isn't really caught year-round. So, when you want to go fishing, you have to ask, "What's running when?" Folks who live and work in coastal communities know the answer almost instinctively, but for the rest of us it takes practice. You can also always ask your local seafood expert. And remember, previously frozen fish isn't a bad thing. The following list of fish runs has been compiled with information from North Carolina Sea Grant, Locals Seafood, and the North Carolina Wildlife Federation.

SPRING	SUMMER	FALL	WINTER
amberjack	amberjack	clams	catfish
bluefish	bluefish	conch	clams
clams	butterfish (harvestfish)	crab	croaker
grouper	clams	croaker	dogfish
lionfish	grouper	flounder	flounder
monkfish	ribbonfish	hogfish (pigfish)	monkfish
porgy (joltfish)	sea mullet (whiting)	mullet	oysters
snapper	shrimp	mackerel	porgy (joltfish)
soft-shell crab	snapper	oysters	sea trout (speckled trout)
tuna	sugar toad	sea mullet (whiting)	rockfish (striped bass)
	swordfish	sea trout	white grunt
	tripletail	sheepshead	
	tuna	shrimp	
		spot	
		sugar toad	
		swordfish	
		white perch	

Helpful Kitchen Equipment

You can certainly cook fish with whatever equipment you already have, but these tools might be helpful.

- » Fish spatula
- » Wire-mesh strainer or spider skimmer
- » Sharp fillet knife
- » Heavy-bottomed stockpot
- » Counter fryer or Dutch oven
- » Candy/deep fry thermometer

Sources for Fish and Know-How

These are my go-to suppliers and resources for buying and learning about local North Carolina seafood.

- » Salty Catch Seafood Company: saltycatchseafood.com
- » Murray L. Nixon Fishery: nixonfishery.com
- » Sunburst Trout Farm: sunbursttrout.com
- » Locals Seafood: localsseafood.com
- » NC Catch: nccatch.org
- » North Carolina Wildlife Resources Commission (licensing, permits, and regulations): ncwildlife.org

Standard Operating Procedure

STOCKS, SEASONINGS, AND SAUCES

Fish Stock **31**

Shellfish Stock **32**

"Joint" Seasoning **33**

Spice Boil Seasoning **34**

Spiced Fish Rub **35**

Cocktail Sauce **36**

Tartar Sauce **37**

Cold Mustard-Herb Sauce **38**

Simple Hot Sauce **39**

All-Purpose (AP) Seafood Dredge **40**

In the army, we had to have everything in state of readiness. In culinary school, they teach *mise en place*, which literally means "everything in its place and a place for everything." Every step of the way, I've been taught the importance of having all of your essential items ready and available in order to prepare a dish from start to finish. In this chapter, I pass along these skills to you.

Part of successful cooking is preparing the fundamental components to complete the dish. Going through that process also gives you a new level of appreciation. You may never have considered how little time it takes to make such fundamentals as stocks and sauces, but you likely have the base ingredients for them in your pantry. These scratch-made items are not hard to prepare (I wouldn't include the recipes if they were).

These homemade essentials are even more important when you are creating a local dish. If you're going to the fishmonger and purchasing fresh, local catch, it makes sense to get the best value for your money. That means using the whole fish, including the bones and other inedible parts to make something else such as a homemade stock. And why stop there? With a little effort you can make other fundamental components—sauces, stocks, seasonings, and more—from scratch. Honestly, it's just as important as using fresh local seafood.

Fish Stock

The foundation of a good seafood soup or stew is a good fish stock.

Makes 6 cups
....

2 pounds fish bones and heads, rinsed and gills removed

6 cups water

1 cup dry white wine

1 medium leek, thinly sliced

1 medium white onion, thinly sliced

1 medium celery stalk, thinly sliced

1 large garlic clove, coarsely chopped

1 bunch of fresh parsley

4 sprigs of fresh thyme

3 bay leaves

1 teaspoon whole black peppercorns

1 teaspoon sea salt

Combine all the ingredients in a large stockpot set over medium-low heat and simmer, uncovered, for 30 minutes. Strain the stock through 2 layers of moistened cheesecloth and discard the solids.

The stock can be refrigerated overnight or frozen for 1 month.

Shellfish Stock

Unlike white fish bones, crustacean shells don't provide the gelatin that helps thicken stock. When you want to make a shellfish stock, you'll need to fortify it with a base of Fish Stock.

Makes about 2¾ quarts

....

3 tablespoons extra-virgin olive oil

3 pounds crustacean shells

1 tablespoon tomato paste

1 medium celery stalk, thinly sliced

1 small leek, whites and pale green parts only, trimmed, washed, and thinly sliced

2 plum tomatoes, roughly chopped

1 small yellow onion, peeled and thinly sliced

1 small carrot, peeled, trimmed, and thinly sliced

1 cup dry white wine (such as Pinot Grigio or Sauvignon Blanc)

3 quarts Fish Stock (page 31)

1 whole large garlic clove

1 bay leaf

1 small bouquet of fresh thyme, tarragon, and parsley

Heat the oil in a large stockpot set over medium-high heat. When the oil shimmers, add the crustacean shells and cook, stirring occasionally, for about 15 minutes. Add the tomato paste and cook, stirring, for 1–2 minutes. Add the celery, leeks, tomatoes, onions, and carrots and cook, stirring often, until the vegetables are soft. Add the remaining ingredients and bring the mixture to a boil, skimming off any foam that rises to the surface. Reduce the heat to medium and simmer, partially covered, for 30 minutes. Strain the stock through a colander, discard the solids, and then strain again through a cheesecloth-lined sieve. Cover and store the strained stock in the refrigerator until ready to use. It will keep for 3–5 days in the refrigerator or 6 months in the freezer.

"Joint" Seasoning

This seasoning is good for any seafood preparation.

Makes about ¼ cup
. . . .

2 tablespoons smoked sweet paprika

1 teaspoon ground coriander

1 teaspoon lemon powder (such as TrueLemon)

1 teaspoon ground fennel

1 teaspoon granulated garlic

1 teaspoon salt

1 teaspoon freshly cracked black pepper

½ teaspoon cayenne pepper

Combine all the ingredients and store in an airtight container in a cool, dark place. This seasoning will stay fresh for 3 months if sealed well.

Spice Boil Seasoning

The perfect seasoning for all kinds of seafood boils.

Makes about 1 cup
....

½ cup pickling spices
¼ cup sea salt
2 tablespoons mustard seeds
2 tablespoons whole black peppercorns
2 tablespoons crushed red pepper
1 tablespoon celery seeds
1 tablespoon dried thyme
2 teaspoons dried oregano
2 teaspoons ground coriander
3 bay leaves

Pulse all the ingredients in a food processor until the mixture forms a coarse powder. Store in an airtight container in a cool, dark place for up to 3 months.

Spiced Fish Rub

This spice rub works well with grilled, broiled, or roasted fish. Sprinkle it generously all over the fish to create a robust and flavorful crust.

Makes just under ¼ cup

....

1 teaspoon garlic powder

1 teaspoon salt

½ teaspoon smoked sweet paprika

½ teaspoon ground fennel

½ teaspoon ground coriander

½ teaspoon dried dill

½ teaspoon dried thyme

½ teaspoon ground ginger

⅛ teaspoon cayenne pepper

⅛ teaspoon freshly cracked black pepper

Combine all the ingredients and store in an airtight container in a cool, dark place for up to 3 months.

Cocktail Sauce

Once you make this simple sauce, you'll never want to buy bottled again.

Makes about 2 cups

....

2 cups ketchup
2 tablespoons light brown sugar
1 tablespoon steak sauce
1 tablespoon fresh lemon juice
2 teaspoons Worcestershire sauce
2 teaspoons horseradish, or to taste
Salt and freshly cracked black pepper to taste

Combine all the ingredients, cover, and refrigerate until ready to use. It will keep for 2 weeks in the refrigerator.

Tartar Sauce

This tangy sauce can be made up to a week in advance.

Makes about 2 cups

....

1 small shallot, finely chopped
1 medium garlic clove, finely grated
1 cup mayonnaise (preferably Duke's)
½ cup finely chopped hard-boiled eggs
2 tablespoons finely chopped capers
2 tablespoons finely chopped sweet pickles
1 tablespoon finely chopped fresh chives
1 tablespoon finely chopped fresh parsley
1 tablespoon fresh lemon juice
1 teaspoon hot sauce (preferably Texas Pete)
1 teaspoon whole grain mustard
Salt and freshly cracked pepper to taste

Whisk all the ingredients together, cover, and refrigerate until ready to use.

Cold Mustard-Herb Sauce

This sauce, traditionally served with snow and blue crab cocktail claws, is a wonderful addition to your arsenal of seafood condiments.

Makes about 2 cups
....

1 cup mayonnaise (preferably Duke's)
¼ cup sour cream
¼ cup prepared horseradish
¼ cup clam juice
¼ cup Dijon mustard
1 tablespoon yellow mustard
1 tablespoon chopped fresh dill
1 tablespoon chopped fresh parsley
1 teaspoon hot sauce (preferably Texas Pete)
1 teaspoon fresh lemon juice

Whisk all the ingredients together, cover, and refrigerate until ready to use.

Simple Hot Sauce

This sauce is a good weekend project. Be sure to cook it in a well-ventilated area.

Makes about 2 cups
....

20 serrano peppers or 12 very ripe red jalapeño peppers (about 10 ounces),
     stems and seeds removed and cut crosswise into ⅛-inch slices
¾ cup thinly sliced yellow onion
1½ tablespoons finely chopped garlic
1 teaspoon vegetable oil
¾ teaspoon salt, plus more to taste
2 cups water
1 cup distilled white vinegar

Combine the peppers, onions, garlic, oil, and salt in a nonreactive saucepan set over high heat and sauté until the onions are translucent, about 3 minutes.

Add the water and cook, stirring occasionally, until the peppers are very soft and almost all the liquid has evaporated, about 20 minutes. *Note*: This should be done in a very well-ventilated area!

Remove the saucepan from the heat and steep the mixture until it comes to room temperature.

Purée the mixture in a food processor for 15 seconds. With the food processor running, add the vinegar through the feed tube in a steady stream until the mixture is smooth. Season with salt.

Carefully strain the mixture through 2 layers of cheesecloth or a fine-mesh sieve and then transfer the sauce to a sterilized pint jar or bottle, secure it with an airtight lid, and refrigerate. Age the sauce for at least 2 weeks before using. It will keep for 6 months in the refrigerator.

All-Purpose (AP) Seafood Dredge

Use this dredge for all of your fish and shellfish frying preparations.

Makes about 2¼ cups
....

2 cups fine yellow corn flour
2 tablespoons dried parsley
1 tablespoon celery powder
1 tablespoon salt
2 teaspoons freshly cracked black pepper
2 teaspoons sweet paprika
1 teaspoon onion powder
1 teaspoon garlic powder
1 teaspoon sour salt (citric acid)
½ teaspoon cayenne pepper
½ teaspoon dry yellow mustard

Combine all the ingredients and store in an airtight container labeled "AP Seafood Dredge."

FISH GREASE VERSUS OTHER GREASE
When you fry a bone fish, those seafood flavors infuse the cooking oil. You should save this oil, called "grease," to use for future fish fries. Back in the day, a lot of households did this, and it just made sense not to get rid of it, particularly if it wasn't burnt. But you didn't want your chicken to taste like fish, so you also had separate stored greases for each kind of fried foods. Everything was organized right by the stove: bacon, chicken, and fish. Over time, Crisco and other generic brands of vegetable shortening transitioned from using aluminum containers to plastic ones. Instead, you could go to regional department stores like Crest (very old-school) and buy little metal cans with built-in strainers made for grease. I still have these cans in my home kitchen organized next to the stove.

Fried and Joy

PAN-FRYING AND DEEP-FRYING

Ritz Cracker–Crusted Bluefish Cakes **43**

Pan-Fried Oyster Dressing Cakes **45**

My Crab Cakes **47**

Shallow-Fried Bone-In Pan Fish **49**

Saltbox's Famous Shrimp Roll **50**

Deep-Fried Hard-Shell Blue Crabs **51**

Scallop Fritters **52**

Fried Salt, Pepper, and Jalapeño Squid **53**

Chicken-Fried Sugar Toads **55**

Fried Seafood Platter with Salsa Criolla (*Jalea*) **56**

All up and down Highway 70 from New Bern to Riverdale folks celebrate their shared cultural heritage of fried fish and hard crabs. It's a regional thing: generally when I mention it to people who don't come from Down East, they aren't familiar with the preparation. At some point in history, someone must have said, "We should fry these things! It's the same finished product as steaming, but then you get to eat the whole thing!" In this chapter, I show you how to fry these and other seafoods perfectly. The more you practice, the more perfect your pan-frying and deep-frying will be.

Growing up, we used to go crabbing along the Neuse River for hard blue crabs, No. 1 jimmies (the meatiest male crabs), measuring 5½ inches from point to point. We didn't go to the market to get them as you might nowadays, and they were a luxury, too, because in order to catch them, you had to sacrifice chicken necks and backs, which were usually saved for frying up.

There was a place in downtown New Bern, right behind Tryon Palace, where the road curved around the river bend and green metal rails kept the traffic and pedestrians from failing into the water. In the summer my friends and I, a group of little rascals of twelve to fourteen, would get some string and fish heads, chicken necks, or whatever was available and go crabbing on that section of road. We'd start out early in the morning before it got too hot. Our tools were a bucket, some string, and a net. We would secure the fish heads on the strings so that the crabs couldn't pull them off, then we'd throw our lines far into the water and wait. Once you saw the string move it was time to pull it in, slow and steady, or the crab would jump off the line. One of us would hang off the green rail pulling the string, while another leaned over with a net dipped into the water to catch the crab and put it in the bucket. On a good day, we could catch three or four dozen.

We carried our bucket of crabs back home and somebody, always a parent or an aunt or an uncle, would help to clean them. The adults were very particular, and everything had to be sanitized just so. After a quick knife to the brain, the back shell was removed, the dead man's fingers (gray-colored gills) were pulled out, and the whole crab was soaked in salt water to remove any impurities. Everybody else got to work prepping the batter and the oil. In my family, crabs were always fried up hard, never steamed. Each crab was dipped in a pancake-y batter—a sort of a tempura-esque, thin, and slightly sweet dip usually made of Bisquick thinned with water so that it wasn't too cakey—and then liberally dosed with seasoning salt. The adults didn't trust us kids with the frying or the hot oil, so another grownup would fry up the crabs in a skillet of melted Crisco until the batter was crisp.

The fried-hard crust was eaten off the crab or dipped in a bit of apple cider vinegar mixed with salt and pepper. And there was always a bottle of Texas Pete if you wanted some heat. The joy was eating the crabs—you didn't need anything else.

Ritz Cracker–Crusted Bluefish Cakes

Bluefish is very rich and works well when made into cakes. Back home, Ritz crackers were used in all kinds of recipes, from breading for fish and chicken to desserts.

Serves 4

....

8 ounces russet potatoes, peeled and cut into large pieces
½ cup finely chopped yellow onions
½ cup finely chopped green bell peppers
2 tablespoons unsalted butter
1 pound bluefish fillet, skinned
4 tablespoons finely chopped fresh parsley
1 tablespoon Dijon mustard
1 tablespoon all-purpose flour
3 large eggs, well beaten
2 cups Ritz cracker crumbs
4 tablespoons vegetable oil
Salt and freshly cracked black pepper to taste

Bring a large pot of salted water to a boil. Add the potatoes and cook for 15 minutes. Drain and mash the potatoes until smooth.

Melt the butter in a large skillet set over medium heat. Add the onions and green peppers and sauté until soft. Turn off the heat and transfer the vegetables to a large bowl. Wipe the skillet clean.

Return the skillet to medium heat and add the whole bluefish along with enough water to come halfway up the fish. Bring to a boil, then lower the heat, cover, and simmer the fish gently until cooked through, about 5 minutes. Carefully transfer the cooked fish onto a plate. When it is cool enough to handle, use the tines of a fork to flake the fish into large chunks. As you work, be sure to remove any bones.

Mix the fish with the onions and peppers. Add the mashed potatoes, parsley, and mustard and combine. Season the mixture well with salt and pepper and shape it into 4 large patties (6 ounces, or about palm size) or 8 smaller ones (3 ounces).

Pour the flour onto a small plate, the eggs into a shallow bowl, and the cracker crumbs onto a third plate. Gently coat the patties with the flour, dusting off any excess, and then dip them in the eggs. Finally, dip the patties in the cracker crumbs, flipping to coat both sides. Place the patties on a baking sheet and refrigerate for at least 30 minutes.

Heat the oil in a large skillet set over medium heat. When the oil shimmers, add the patties and fry gently, about 5 minutes per side. Carefully remove the cakes from the skillet and drain them on paper towels. Serve immediately.

Pan-Fried Oyster Dressing Cakes

This is not a Thanksgiving dish. This is not a leftover dish. These little cakes stand alone and work best with fresh ingredients from start to finish.

Makes 12 cakes

....

1 pint (about 2 dozen) finely chopped shucked oysters with their liquor

12 ounces stale white bread (6 slices), cut into ½-inch cubes

2 large eggs, well beaten

⅓ cup freshly grated Parmesan

4 tablespoons (½ stick) unsalted butter

3 thick bacon slices, chopped

4 medium celery stalks, chopped

2 tablespoons finely chopped garlic

1 small yellow onion, finely chopped

1 small green bell pepper, finely chopped

1½ cups chicken stock, plus extra for binding

2 tablespoons finely chopped fresh parsley

1 tablespoon finely chopped fresh thyme

2 teaspoons ground coriander

6 fresh sage leaves, finely chopped

Salt and freshly cracked black pepper to taste

Vegetable oil, for frying

Combine the oysters and liquor, bread cubes, eggs, and Parmesan in a large bowl and set aside.

Melt the butter in a heavy skillet set over medium heat. Add the bacon and cook until the fat has rendered and the pieces are cooked through but not crisp, 3–5 minutes.

Add the celery, garlic, onions, and bell peppers, stirring to coat them in the melted fat. Add the stock and simmer until the vegetables are soft, about 10 minutes. Turn off the heat, add the herbs, and mix.

Carefully combine the hot vegetables with the oyster mixture and season with salt and pepper. Cover and refrigerate until chilled through, about 2 hours.

Form the chilled mixture into a dozen 3½-ounce cakes and place them on a platter. Allow the cakes to come to room temperature.

Meanwhile, heat the oil in a heavy-bottomed skillet. Working in batches, fry the cakes, turning once, until browned on both sides and heated through. Carefully remove the cakes from the oil and drain them on paper towels. Serve immediately.

FREEMAN'S BEACH / SEABREEZE

The Jim Crow era enforced the racial segregation of many public places, including specific beaches for summertime recreation. In eastern North Carolina, one of these beaches designated for African American use was also historically settled by a community of freed slaves, which is how it got its original name, Freeman's Beach. Located in Wilmington, Freeman's Beach was also known as Bop City and today is called Seabreeze. Over time this simple strip of undeveloped sand became a lively beach packed with an amusement park that was frequented by entertainers like Count Basie and James Brown as they toured the South on what was called the Chitlin Circuit. Nearby there were also African American watermen and fishermen who would sell their daily catch to beachgoers who would then fry up the fresh, local seafood right there on the shore. This African American cultural heritage endures in foodways along the east coast of North Carolina to this day.

My Crab Cakes

I've enjoyed countless crab cakes in my time, but these are my favorite by far. They are inspired by the best crab cakes you'll find on the Eastern Seaboard, in Oriental, North Carolina. These crab cakes have minimal filler and are made with meat picked from crabs at peak season.

Makes 6 large crab cakes or 24 mini crab cakes
....

1 pound jumbo lump 75% and backfin lump 25% crabmeat, fresh or pasteurized
20 Ritz crackers, finely crushed
1 tablespoon finely chopped fresh parsley
1 tablespoon grated lemon zest
¼ cup mayonnaise (preferably Duke's)
1 large egg
1 tablespoon Dijon mustard
1 tablespoon Worcestershire sauce
4 dashes hot sauce (preferably Texas Pete)
¼ cup canola oil
1 tablespoon unsalted butter

Drain the crabmeat, if necessary, and pick through it for any rogue shells. Combine the crabmeat, cracker crumbs, parsley, and lemon zest in a large bowl, using your fingers to gently break apart some of the lumps.

In another bowl, whisk together the mayonnaise, egg, mustard, Worcestershire sauce, and hot sauce. Add this mixture to the crab mixture, gently stirring to combine. It will be somewhat loose. Cover with plastic wrap and refrigerate for at least 1 hour.

Scoop the chilled crab mixture into six ½-cup mounds and lightly shape them into patties about 1½ inches thick.

Heat the oil in a large skillet set over medium heat. When the oil shimmers, add the crab cakes to the pan. Cook until the undersides are dark golden brown, 4–6 minutes, then flip the cakes. Reduce the heat to medium low and add the butter. Continue to cook until the second sides are browned, 4–6 minutes. Remove the cakes and drain them on paper towels. Serve immediately.

DEFINITION—"CALABASH"

The term "Calabash" refers to the Down East town of the same name. A la Niçoise, A la Calabash! Calabash is a fisherman's town, right on the tip of the border with South Carolina. Folks down in Calabash use only a fine yellow corn flour (not corn meal) when they dredge their seafood for frying. Historically, corn flour was readily available in the area, and so now every restaurant sells the same style of fried fish. Technically, most everybody who fries fish in North Carolina follows the Calabash style. The name can refer to the style of frying as well as to the way the seafood is served, which is typically with slaw and hushpuppies. At Saltbox, by design, we dredge our seafood in simple fine yellow corn flour, in the style of Calabash.

Shallow-Fried Bone-In Pan Fish

This recipe calls for small bone-in pan fish—any fish that can be cooked whole on the bone, such as croaker, spot, whiting, hogfish, and herring. Serve each person two fish.

Serves 6

....

1 cup vegetable oil
12 whole fish, scaled, gutted, gilled, and scored (head on or off,
   per your preference)
Salt and freshly cracked black pepper to taste
4 cups AP Seafood Dredge (page 40)

Heat the oil in a large skillet to 350°.

Wash and pat the fish dry with paper towels.

Season the fish with salt and pepper. Pour the AP Seafood Dredge into a shallow bowl. Dip each fish in the dredge, gently tapping away the excess.

Carefully add a couple of fish to the hot oil and fry until the exposed white meat is opaque, about 5 minutes. Remove the fish and drain them on paper towels. Repeat with the remaining fish. Serve immediately.

Saltbox's Famous Shrimp Roll

This roll combines the concept of the New England lobster roll with that of the southern po'boy and has become a signature seafood sandwich at Saltbox.

Serves 4

. . . .

5 tablespoons unsalted butter, softened
1 teaspoon finely chopped garlic
1 teaspoon grated lemon zest
4 (6-inch) soft rolls, cut like hot-dog buns
Vegetable oil, for deep-frying
¾ cup AP Seafood Dredge (page 40)
2 pounds large shrimp (21/25 count), peeled, deveined, and tails removed
Salt and freshly cracked black pepper to taste
4 tablespoons Saltbox Cocktail and Tartar Sauces (pages 36 and 37)
1 cup Saltbox Bread and Butter Vegetable Slaw (page 115)
4 lemon wedges, for serving

Combine the butter with the garlic and lemon zest and spread it on the inside of each roll. Set aside.

Fill a 2-quart Dutch oven with 3–4 inches of oil and heat the oil to 350°.

Pour the AP Seafood Dredge in a shallow bowl. Season the shrimp with salt and pepper and bread them in the AP Seafood Dredge, gently tapping off the excess.

Carefully add a few shrimp to the hot oil and fry them until they are golden brown, 2–3 minutes. Remove the shrimp with a slotted spoon or a spider skimmer and drain them on paper towels. Continue with the remaining shrimp.

Set a griddle pan over medium heat and toast the rolls, butter-side down, until golden brown.

Spread the Tartar and Cocktail Sauces evenly on all 4 rolls. Divide the shrimp among the rolls and top each roll with a portion of slaw and a lemon wedge.

Deep-Fried Hard-Shell Blue Crabs

Growing up, we only ate hard crabs, so these are my go-to. At the fish market, ask for the crabs to be "dressed" so that they are ready to season, batter, and fry.

Serves 6

....

2 dozen hard-shell blue crabs, cleaned and dressed
1 tablespoon salt, plus more to taste
1 tablespoon freshly cracked black pepper, plus more to taste
2 large eggs
1 cup milk
1 cup lager beer
2 cups AP Seafood Dredge (page 40)
Vegetable oil, for deep-frying

If your crabs have not yet been dressed, remove each crab's outer shell and clean away the eyes, gills, and mustard-colored guts. Rinse the crabs under cold water and pat them dry with paper towels. Keeping the claws and feet attached, split each crab in half with a sharp knife. Season with the salt and pepper.

Fill a large Dutch oven with 3–4 inches of oil and heat the oil to 350°.

In a large bowl, whisk the eggs, milk, beer, and AP Seafood Dredge until smooth.

Working in batches, dip the crabs in the batter, ensuring an even coating. Carefully add a few crabs to the hot oil and fry them until they are golden brown, 5–7 minutes. Remove the crabs, drain them on paper towels, and season with more salt and pepper. Repeat with the remaining crabs.

Scallop Fritters

Expensive sea scallops can be stretched to feed several people when they are fried as fritters.

Makes about 12 fritters
....

Vegetable oil, for frying
½ cup AP Seafood Dredge (page 40)
½ cup all-purpose flour
2 teaspoons baking powder
2 large eggs, lightly beaten
¼ cup lager beer
1 jalapeño pepper, stem and seeds removed and finely chopped
1 small celery stalk, finely chopped
3 scallions, roughly chopped
½ pound roughly chopped sea scallops
Salt and freshly cracked black pepper to taste

Fill a large skillet with 2 inches of oil and heat the oil to 350°.

In a medium bowl, whisk together the AP Seafood Dredge, flour, and baking powder. Add the eggs and beer, whisking until the batter is smooth. Stir in the peppers, celery, scallions, and scallops.

Working in batches, drop heaping tablespoons of the fritter batter into the oil. Fry the fritters, turning them occasionally, until they are golden brown, 6–7 minutes. Carefully remove the fritters with a slotted spoon or a spider skimmer and drain them on paper towels. Season with salt and pepper.

Fried Salt, Pepper, and Jalapeño Squid

This classic Chinese recipe is one of my favorite ways to prepare and eat fried squid. After the squid is fried, it is tossed in a stir-fry of crunchy garlic, ginger, and hot green peppers, which makes this dish extra-special.

Serves 4–6
....

1½ pounds squid

1 tablespoon Shaoxing wine (Chinese rice wine)

½ teaspoon sesame oil

5 cups plus 1 tablespoon vegetable oil, divided

1 cup AP Seafood Dredge (page 40)

1 teaspoon salt, plus more to taste

½ teaspoon freshly cracked white pepper, plus more to taste

2 jalapeño peppers, stems and seeds removed, cut lengthwise,
    and thinly sliced

5 large garlic cloves, thinly sliced

2 teaspoons finely chopped fresh ginger

Prepare the squid: Rinse them well in cold water and pat them dry. Grasp the tentacles of the squid in one hand and the hood (the squid's body) in the other and firmly pull apart. Cut the tentacles off in one piece, separating the tentacles from the head and the innards. Remove the beak (located at the base of the tentacles where they connect to the hood) and discard with the innards. Pull the quill (a thin piece of inedible cartilage) from inside the hood and discard. Slice the hood crosswise to create bite-size rings. Drain the squid pieces in a colander and transfer them to a bowl.

Add the Shaoxing wine and sesame oil to the squid, toss gently, and set aside to marinate.

Heat 5 cups of the oil in a heavy-bottomed pot to 325°.

In a small bowl, combine the AP Seafood Dredge, salt, and pepper. Set aside.

When the oil is hot, working in batches, pick up small fistfuls of squid, squeeze them gently to remove excess liquid, and toss them in the dredge mixture. Carefully lower the dredged squid into the hot oil with a slotted spoon or a spider skimmer. Gently move the pieces back and forth, frying them until they are golden brown, 2–2½ minutes.

Remove the squid and drain them on paper towels. Season with salt and pepper. Fry the remaining pieces in batches.

For the stir-fry, heat the remaining oil in a wok over medium-high heat. Add the ginger and fry for about 20 seconds. Add the garlic, stirring quickly to prevent burning. When the garlic is light golden in color, add the peppers and stir-fry for 30 seconds more. Add the squid and stir-fry quickly in the aromatic mixture for about a minute or so. Transfer the squid to a plate, and don't leave those crispy pieces of garlic and pepper behind! Serve immediately.

DEFINITION—"FRIED HARD"
The southern term "fried hard" refers to seafood cooked to a degree of extreme doneness, that is, extra-crunchy. A lot of people don't like to eat fish that is wet or soft, so you leave it in the oil to fry a little longer to achieve that fried hard texture. If you fry a bone fish hard enough, you can enjoy the crunch of the dorsal fins and everything. At Saltbox, customers always come into the restaurant and ask for a certain fish to be "fried hard." Growing up, my parents cooked and ate fish that way, so we all just ate it that way, too.

Chicken-Fried Sugar Toads

The sugar toad is also known as the Atlantic pufferfish, but don't worry, this species is not lethal. Sugar toads are best eaten with your hands, much as you would eat fried chicken wings.

Serves 4

....

Vegetable oil, for frying
2 cups AP Seafood Dredge (page 40)
1 large egg
1 cup low-fat buttermilk
1 pound sugar toads, cleaned, skin and fins removed
Salt and freshly cracked black pepper to taste
Sea salt, for garnish
Tartar Sauce, for serving (page 37)
Lemon wedges, for garnish

Fill a large cast-iron skillet with 1½ inches of oil and heat the oil to 375°.

Pour the AP Seafood Dredge into a shallow dish. In another shallow dish, whisk together the egg and buttermilk. Season the sugar toads with salt and pepper, dip them in the buttermilk mixture, and then coat them in the AP Seafood Dredge.

When the oil is hot, add a few fish and fry them until they are light brown and crispy, 3–4 minutes. Remove the fish and drain them either on paper towels or on a rack set over a sheet pan. Lightly sprinkle the fish with sea salt. Repeat with the remaining fish. Serve with Tartar Sauce and garnish with lemon wedges.

Fried Seafood Platter with Salsa Criolla (*Jalea*)

This dish is inspired by *jalea*, a coastal Peruvian recipe of fried seafood served with a bright, acidic relish and fried yucca. My version is similar, but I swap the yucca for fried sweet potatoes.

Serves 6

....

FOR THE SALSA CRIOLLA

½ large red onion, thinly sliced

2 medium plum tomatoes, diced

¼ cup loosely packed, chopped cilantro leaves and tender stems

1 fresh aji amarillo pepper, stem removed, seeded, and finely chopped

1 medium garlic clove, finely chopped

2 tablespoons extra-virgin olive oil

¼ cup fresh lime juice

Salt and freshly cracked black pepper to taste

FOR THE FRIED SEAFOOD

1½–2 quarts vegetable oil

4 cups AP Seafood Dredge, divided (page 40)

¾ cup cornstarch

1½ teaspoons baking powder

1½ teaspoons salt, plus more to taste

¾ teaspoon freshly cracked black pepper, plus more to taste

½ teaspoon sweet paprika

2 cups lager beer, divided

½ pound firm white-fleshed fish, such as flounder, grouper, or sheepshead, skinned, boned, and sliced into 1½-by-1-inch pieces

½ pound large shrimp (21/25 count), shelled, deveined, and tail removed

⅓ pound freshly shucked oysters

In a large bowl, combine all the ingredients for the salsa and let it sit at room temperature, stirring occasionally, until the onions soften slightly and turn bright pink, about 10 minutes. Drain well, cover, and set aside.

Preheat the oven to 400°. Heat the oil in a deep-fryer, medium pot, or wok to 350°.

In a large bowl, whisk together 1½ cups of the AP Seafood Dredge, cornstarch, baking powder, salt, black pepper, and paprika. Whisk in 1½ cups of the beer to form a thick batter; some small lumps of flour are okay.

Pour the remaining AP Seafood Dredge into a shallow bowl.

Gently coat the fish pieces in the dredge, shake off the excess, and transfer to the beer batter, turning to coat. Pick up the fish and allow any excess batter to drip back into the bowl (a wire strainer can be helpful with this). Return the fish to the dredge and coat quickly on all sides, tapping gently to remove any excess. Repeat with the remaining pieces.

Working in batches, carefully lower the fish into the hot oil and fry, agitating and turning frequently, until golden brown, about 3 minutes. Transfer the fish to a large bowl lined with paper towels and season with salt, shaking gently to release excess oil. Place the fish on a rack set over a baking sheet.

Increase the oil temperature to 375°. Repeat the dredging and battering process with the shrimp and fry them in batches until they are golden, 2–3 minutes. Transfer the shrimp to the large bowl lined with fresh paper towels and season with salt, shaking gently to release excess oil. Place the shrimp on the rack with the fish.

Whisk the remaining beer into the batter until thoroughly incorporated (this thins the batter slightly, making the oysters easier to work with). Repeat the dredging and battering process with the oysters. Fry until golden brown, about 2 minutes. Transfer to the same large bowl again lined with fresh paper towels and season with salt. Shake gently to release excess oil. Place the oysters on the rack with the fish and shrimp.

To serve, mound the fried seafood on a large plate. Arrange the salsa on top and serve the dish immediately with fried sweet potatoes.

Into the Coals

GRILLING, SMOKING, AND CHARCOALING

Broiled Green-Tail Shrimp with Bay Leaf Butter **61**

Broiled Panko-and-Herb-Crusted Triggerfish **63**

Grilled or Broiled Oysters with Carolina Treet Butter **64**

Grilled Dogfish with Red Jalapeño Rub **65**

Griddled Amberjack Collars with Fresh Thyme **66**

Smoky Deviled Bluefish **67**

Hickory Charcoal Mullet with BBQ Butter **68**

Salt-and-Pepper Charcoal Sea Scallops **69**

Smoked Mullet with Cider-Sorghum Syrup Glaze **70**

Whole Roasted Fish on the Bone with Salsa Verde **72**

Growing up, we never grilled fish. It was all fried. Period. When I left home, I began to understand and enjoy cooking over an open flame. Then, in culinary school, we smoked trout, and I learned how smoking and curing have evolved from necessary methods of food preservation into something fancier that we now learn as culinary arts.

This chapter combines the three techniques of grilling, smoking, and curing because contemporary preparations typically use a charcoal or gas grill. It's important, however, to acknowledge their culinary and historical differences.

Grilling, likely the most familiar to us all, is a method in which raw ingredients are cooked with dry heat, generally over an open flame (except when you use something like an indoor grill pan). Smoking is a slower process that uses smoke (most often from wood) to flavor, cook, and preserve raw ingredients. And curing is a preservation technique that relies on the curative properties of some combination of salt, sugar, and smoke. This chapter pays homage to all three traditional North Carolina culinary methods.

Down East is a historically Indigenous area. The lands and waterways up and down Highway 70—like the Croatan National Forest and the Pamlico Sound—are named after the people who settled there long ago. From a North Carolina point of view, smoked and grilled fish are Native American traditions. People would take a local whole fish like jumping mullet, butterfly it open, skewer it on stakes, and grill it over a straight line of hot coals. The open fire would make the skin perfectly crisp. Nowadays, we call this charcoal mullet and serve it with hushpuppies and coleslaw. I season my version with a barbecue dressing, and when it's ready you can eat it whole, right out of the charcoal-charred skin.

Grilling fish was a communal activity and usually marked a special event, though it didn't necessarily mean anything too complicated. The best version subtracts all the fancy ingredients and uses the freshest fish you can get. And even though traditional methods for charcoal mullet and other grilled fish require an open flame, you can make this dish on a regular outdoor grill or a kitchen grill pan.

Broiled Green-Tail Shrimp with Bay Leaf Butter

You always hear about putting Old Bay Seasoning on seafood, but I prefer to use one of my favorite simple seasonings, ground bay leaf.

Serves 4

....

Juice of ½ lemon
4 large garlic cloves, crushed
5 tablespoons roughly chopped fresh parsley
2 tablespoons roughly chopped fresh dill
1 tablespoon ground bay leaf
6 tablespoons (¾ stick) unsalted butter, softened
Salt and freshly cracked black pepper to taste
24 medium green-tail (white) shrimp, peeled and deveined
Lemon wedges and crusty bread, for serving

In a medium bowl, form a paste with the lemon juice, garlic, parsley, dill, ground bay leaf, and butter. Season well with salt and pepper.

Spread the shrimp on a large baking sheet. Gently spread the paste evenly over the shrimp and marinate it at room temperature for 30 minutes.

Preheat the broiler to medium high. Broil the shrimp for 5–6 minutes. Spoon the shrimp along with the pan juices onto a warm plate. Serve with lemon wedges and crusty bread.

A BAKE IS REALLY A BOIL

Despite its confusing name, a seafood bake alludes to a shoreside or beachside cooking event for a large group of people that typically involves fresh seafood, an open fire, a giant stockpot, and a lot of boiling liquid. When you're on the beach, driftwood or other wood scraps are used to build a fire and the giant stockpot is leveled over the flames or on a metal grate. The pot is fitted with a perforated metal steamer basket that allows you to pull everything out when it's cooked. Ingredients can be all-purpose, but they typically include seafood, corn on the cob, sausage, potatoes, and some sort of bay seasoning for the cooking liquid. Traditionally, an eastern North Carolina clambake also contains waterfowl such as seabirds or ducks, but I prefer to use chicken. When ready, the contents of the pot are dumped on a table. Diners pile the bake on paper plates and dip the seafood in drawn butter with their fingers. In North Carolina, clams are in season during the fall and in wintertime, so traditional clambakes on the beach are best after Labor Day.

Broiled Panko-and-Herb-Crusted Triggerfish

Triggerfish has a thick, leathery skin and requires a bit of skill to clean, so be sure to have your fishmonger prepare the fish for you.

Serves 4–6

....

7 tablespoons unsalted butter, melted, divided
2 (1-pound) triggerfish fillets
1 teaspoon salt, plus more to taste
Freshly cracked black pepper to taste
½ cup panko
3 tablespoons coarsely chopped flat-leaf parsley
6 sprigs of fresh thyme, leaves only, finely chopped
Finely grated zest of 1 orange
Finely grated zest of 1 lemon

Preheat the broiler to medium and line a baking sheet with foil. Grease the foil lightly with 1 tablespoon of the butter.

Place the fish on the greased baking sheet and season all over with salt and pepper. Allow the fish to rest at room temperature for 20 minutes.

In a small bowl, stir together the panko, parsley, thyme, orange and lemon zests, 1 teaspoon of the salt, and the remaining melted butter.

Sprinkle the panko topping evenly over the fish. Broil the fish until the topping is browned and the fish flakes when the center is poked with a fork, 7–9 minutes. Serve immediately.

Grilled or Broiled Oysters with Carolina Treet Butter

I wish more people would grill or broil oysters. It's so easy, and the quick blast of heat concentrates the oysters' natural briny flavor.

Makes 24 oysters
....

4 tablespoons (½ stick) unsalted butter, softened
1 teaspoon Carolina Treet Cooking Barbecue Sauce
1 teaspoon finely chopped shallots
1 teaspoon finely chopped garlic
1 tablespoon fresh lime juice
¼ teaspoon salt
2 teaspoons finely chopped cilantro
24 oysters on the half shell

Combine the butter, Carolina Treet sauce, shallots, garlic, lime juice, salt, and cilantro in a small bowl and chill.

Prepare the grill or preheat the broiler for high heat.

Top each oyster with a dollop of the chilled butter. Place the oysters, shell down, on the grill or in the broiler and cook for 3–4 minutes. Carefully remove the hot oysters with a pair of tongs or a wide metal spatula and arrange them on a plate to serve. *Caution:* The shells will be very hot!

Grilled Dogfish with Red Jalapeño Rub

There are two species of dogfish—smooth and spiny—and both are considered sand sharks. When I first put dogfish on the Saltbox menu, my patrons were skeptical, but I used to joke with them and say, "If you can eat catfish, why wouldn't you try dogfish?"

Serves 8

....

6 large garlic cloves, finely chopped and mashed into a paste
5 red jalapeño peppers, stems removed, seeded, and finely chopped
4 tablespoons ground cumin, toasted
4 tablespoons finely chopped fresh mint
4 tablespoons extra-virgin olive oil, divided, plus more for the grill
Salt to taste
8 (7-ounce) dogfish fillets

Combine the garlic, peppers, cumin, and mint in a small bowl and set aside. Prepare the grill for medium-high heat and season the grates with oil.

Rub 2 tablespoons of the oil all over the fish fillets and season liberally with salt. Place the fillets in a grill basket.

Transfer the basket of fish to the grill and sprinkle the fillets with half of the jalapeño mixture. Grill, uncovered, until golden, about 4 minutes. Flip the fish and drizzle the fillets with the remaining oil, then sprinkle them with the remaining jalapeño mixture. Grill until the fillets are cooked through, 4–5 minutes more. Serve immediately.

Griddled Amberjack Collars with Fresh Thyme

Certain fish species are prized for their collars, or the throat area just below the gills. When cooked, this triangular piece of flesh looks a lot like a chicken thigh.

Serves 4

....

⅓ cup extra-virgin olive oil
2 teaspoons salt
2 teaspoons freshly cracked black pepper
2 teaspoons grated lemon zest
2 small bunches of fresh thyme
4 large garlic cloves, thinly sliced
4 amberjack collars, skin removed
Lemon wedges, for serving

Combine the oil, salt, pepper, lemon zest, thyme, and garlic in a bowl. Place the collars in large, heavy-duty zip-top bags and divide the seasoned oil equally among the bags. Seal and shake the bags to coat the collars thoroughly. Chill for at least 1 hour or overnight.

Prepare the grill for high heat. Arrange the collars in a single layer, not touching, and grill with the cover open until they are slightly charred, about 5 minutes. Gently turn the fish and grill the other side until the flesh is flaky and cooked through. Serve hot with lemon wedges.

Smoky Deviled Bluefish

If you like blackened fish, this is the perfect North Carolina version with my go-to spice mixture. At Saltbox, whenever people ask for a fish to be blackened, this is what I recommend.

Serves 4

....

4 (7-ounce) boneless, skin-on bluefish fillets
¼ cup extra-virgin olive oil
2 tablespoons Aleppo pepper, divided
1 tablespoon garlic powder, divided
1 tablespoon grated lemon zest
1 tablespoon smoked sweet paprika
1 tablespoon Worcestershire sauce
2 teaspoons Dijon mustard
Salt and freshly cracked black pepper to taste
Lemon wedges, for serving

Place the fish in a 9 × 13-inch baking dish.

In a small bowl, stir together the oil, 1 tablespoon of the Aleppo pepper, ½ tablespoon of the garlic powder, lemon zest, paprika, Worcestershire sauce, mustard, salt, and pepper to form a paste. Rub the paste all over the fish, cover the fish with plastic wrap, and chill for 1 hour.

Heat a charcoal grill or set a gas grill to medium high. Using paper towels, wipe off the excess paste from the fish and season the fillets with salt and pepper. Carefully transfer the fillets to the grill, and cook, flipping once, until they are cooked through and slightly charred, 3–5 minutes. Remove the fish from the grill and sprinkle with the remaining Aleppo pepper and garlic powder. Serve with lemon wedges.

Hickory Charcoal Mullet with BBQ Butter

Charcoal mullet is a signature Down East specialty. Every fall, folks eagerly await the seasonal mullet blow: when the nor'easter winds start to blow, schools of mullet follow, and the season begins.

Serves 4–6
....

1 pound (4 sticks) unsalted butter, at room temperature

2 tablespoons apple cider vinegar

1 tablespoon distilled white vinegar

1 tablespoon honey

1 tablespoon Pepsi

2 teaspoons crushed red pepper

1 teaspoon freshly cracked black pepper

1 teaspoon salt

4 pounds striped mullet fillets, scaled and skinned with the belly left on

6 tablespoons Spiced Fish Rub (page 35)

Combine the softened butter, cider and white vinegars, honey, Pepsi, crushed red pepper, black pepper, and salt in a small bowl and set aside.

Start a medium-hot hickory wood charcoal fire in a grill.

Wash, rinse, and pat dry the mullet fillets and season them liberally with the Spiced Fish Rub on both sides.

Lightly oil the grill grates, place the seasoned fillets skin-side down, and cover with the lid. After 5 minutes, brush the fillets with the BBQ butter.

Place the cover back on and cook the mullet until the scales and skin become charred and the mullet fat starts bubbling, about 5 minutes more.

Before taking the fillets off the grill, brush them with more BBQ butter, then serve hot.

Salt-and-Pepper Charcoal Sea Scallops

The freshness of the scallops is the essence of this dish. Cooking the scallops over hot coals adds a nice smoky flavor.

Serves 4
....

16 large sea scallops, side muscles removed
2 tablespoons extra-virgin olive oil, plus more for the grill and for finishing
Salt and freshly cracked black pepper to taste
Lemon wedges, for serving

Prepare a grill for medium-high heat and oil the grates well.

On a baking sheet, toss the scallops with 2 tablespoons of the oil and season with salt and pepper. Using a fish spatula or your hands, place the scallops on the grill, flat side down. Grill, turning once, until lightly charred and just cooked through, about 2 minutes per side. Dress the scallops with fresh lemon and a drizzle of olive oil.

SMOKED FISH
When I first opened Saltbox and found that a fish on the menu wasn't selling as fast as I'd like, I would cover it in a dry cure made with salt, pepper, sugar, chilis, citrus, and herbs, rinse it clean, then slowly smoke it. I'd serve it like this or pull the flesh off the bones and mix it into a spread to go on crackers or toast. I found this method useful in helping folks overcome negative expectations of certain fish. While there's nothing new about smoking or smoked fish, the presentation of smoked local North Carolina seafood is new for a lot of modern eaters. Folks are already familiar with the smoking methods of North Carolina barbecue and we've got smoker pits everywhere. We are already well established as a smoked-foods state, so it shouldn't be too difficult to make some space for smoked fish in our regional foodways.

Smoked Mullet with Cider-Sorghum Syrup Glaze

The striped or jumping mullet is also known as hardhead, popeye, and roundhead mullet. But whatever you call it, this fish is best when smoked.

Serves 6–8
....

2 gallons water, divided, plus more for soaking the wood chips

1¼ cups salt

½ cup firmly packed light brown sugar

3 tablespoons freshly cracked black pepper

2 tablespoons dried thyme

8 bay leaves

¼ cup hot sauce (preferably Texas Pete)

4 (1-pound) mullets, scaled, gutted, heads removed, and butterflied

1 large yellow onion, coarsely chopped

1 tablespoon whole black peppercorns

¼ cup apple cider vinegar

¾ cup sorghum

3 tablespoons finely chopped shallots

2 sprigs of fresh thyme

¾ teaspoon freshly cracked black pepper

1–2 teaspoons vegetable oil

Make a brine. In a large container, combine 1 gallon of the water, salt, brown sugar, black pepper, dried thyme, bay leaves, and hot sauce. Stir to dissolve the salt and sugar. Add the fish, cover with plastic wrap, and chill for 48 hours.

Soak the wood chips in a bucket of water for 2–3 hours, then drain. Prepare a home smoker according to the wood chip manufacturer's directions and place the soaked chips in the bottom tray.

In the upper container of the smoker, combine the remaining gallon of water with the onions and peppercorns. Cover the smoker and let the fire burn for 30 minutes.

In a small saucepan, make a glaze by combining the vinegar, sorghum, shallots, thyme, and black pepper. Simmer the glaze to reduce the volume by a fourth. Remove the pan from the heat, let cool, and set aside.

Lightly coat the grill with vegetable oil.

Remove the fish from the brine and pat them dry inside and out. Gently brush both sides of each fish with the glaze.

Place the fish on the grill above the water and cook, covered, turning once, until crisp and the skin is dry, about 1–1¼ hours. Remove the fish from the smoker and serve either hot or chilled.

Whole Roasted Fish on the Bone with Salsa Verde

Wow your guests with this wonderfully simple way to cook whole fish on the bone complete with an impressive presentation that calls for fresh herbs and citrus.

Serves 4

....

FOR THE SALSA VERDE

½ cup finely chopped fresh parsley

¼ cup finely chopped fresh basil

¼ cup finely chopped fresh mint

1 tablespoon minced capers

1 teaspoon red wine vinegar

1 medium garlic clove, finely chopped

½ jalapeño pepper, stem and seeds removed and finely chopped (optional)

1 cup extra-virgin olive oil

2 tablespoons fresh lemon juice

Salt and freshly cracked black pepper to taste

FOR THE FISH

1 (2½-pound) whole red snapper, black bass, porgy, or rosefish, cleaned and scaled

2 tablespoons extra-virgin olive oil

Salt and freshly cracked black pepper to taste

1 lemon, thinly sliced

¼ cup chopped mixed fresh herbs, such as thyme, oregano, parsley, and rosemary

1 medium shallot, thinly sliced

¼ fennel bulb, thinly sliced

3 garlic cloves, crushed

Combine all the ingredients for the salsa verde in a medium bowl and set aside.

Preheat the oven to 450° and line a baking sheet with parchment paper.

Place the fish on the baking sheet. Using a sharp knife, make 3 crosswise slashes down to the bone on each side of the fish. Rub the fish with the oil and season with salt and pepper. Stuff each slash with 1 lemon slice and a big pinch of the mixed herbs. Stuff the cavity of the fish with the shallots, fennel, garlic, and remaining lemon slices and herbs. Roast until the flesh is opaque, about 20 minutes. Serve hot with salsa verde on the side.

One-Pots

SOUPS, CHOWDERS, AND STEWS

Hot-Smoked Trout and Sour Corn Chowda **77**

Core Sound Clam and Sweet Potato Chowder **79**

Monkfish Chowder with Sea Beans and Dill **81**

"Warsh"-Pot Fish Stew **83**

Core Sound Clams with Gold Tomato and Corn Broth **85**

Cedar Island Fish Pie **87**

River Camp Fish Muddle **89**

North River Camp Clambake **91**

Stewed Clams and Country Sausage **92**

Singapore-Style Fish Collar Curry **94**

In eastern North Carolina, we use the term "stew" a lot. We also use "stewed," "stew fried," and "stewed whole." The thing to remember is that it all goes in the pot, as I teach you in this chapter. The act of stewing lends itself to bits and pieces of fish, including the bones and the trimmings, as well as to whole durable fish (like red drum, the state fish of North Carolina).

Washpot stew is a traditional wintertime dish in eastern North Carolina. This dish is made with rockfish, which spawn in river communities all along the East Coast. Back in the day, this stew was cooked in a cast-iron washpot over an open fire. When the season was right, folk would catch some fish, bring them home, and the spread the word that a stew would be going soon. This concept of rural, informal food is the foundation of Down East cooking. You knew when certain fish were running and where to catch them. Others would join in with coolers of beer to come shoot the breeze and eat fresh fish stew. The basic recipe calls for salt pork or bacon, onions, water, Campbell's tomato soup, potatoes, seasoning, salt and pepper, and rockfish layered in large, steaklike cuts. The head goes in, too. Once everything is cooked through, the potatoes are fork-tender, and the fish is gently moist and loose, then whole eggs are cracked open and eased into the stewing liquid to poach. The whole thing is served with plain, sliced white bread.

When I opened Saltbox, I did this dish very chefy, with carefully layered potatoes and leeks and a homemade bone stock. I added just enough liquid to cover the fish and vegetable layers, then put the dish into the oven to poach gently. And even though this elevated version was executed perfectly, I still love to make the traditional recipe with the giant pot bubbling away. I later bought myself the largest pot I could find, specifically for making washpot stew. Then I found a giant wooden spoon (about two and a half feet long) at a Mexican grocery store over in Durham to go with the washpot.

This method of one-pot cooking extends to countless iterations of stew, soup, and chowder recipes traditional to eastern North Carolina cuisine. Although the recipes may differ slightly from county to county, they rely on the same basic principles. They are generally served with white bread or corn dodgers (corn dumplings cooked on top of the hot liquid). Down East we always use some sort of pork to start the dish, and we prefer to finish without heavy dairy (Hatteras clam chowder, for instance, has no cream). Last, and probably most important, these one-pot dishes absolutely must use fresh, local seafood, preferably bone-in to infuse more flavor as the dish slowly simmers on the stove.

Hot-Smoked Trout and Sour Corn Chowda

Trout start running in autumn. This chowder is the perfect way to start the season.

Serves 4

....

FOR THE SOUR CORN

12 ears sweet corn

1 quart springwater

3 tablespoons pickling salt

1 bay leaf

1 cinnamon stick

1 dried red chili pod

FOR THE CHOWDER

2 tablespoons unsalted butter

1 medium yellow onion, finely chopped

1 small celery stalk, finely diced

2 russet potatoes, diced into bite-size pieces

1½ cups Sour Corn (recipe above)

1 cup boiling water

12 ounces hot-smoked trout fillet, skinned and flaked (I prefer the
     hot-smoked trout from Sunburst Trout Farm)

1¼ cups heavy cream

Salt and freshly cracked black pepper to taste

2 tablespoons finely chopped fresh chives, for garnish

Using a sharp knife, cut the kernels from the cobs and reserve the corn, discarding the cobs.

In a large bowl, combine the springwater and salt and stir to dissolve the salt.

In a large glass jar or ceramic crock, combine the corn kernels with the spices and then pour the brine on top. Keep the corn submerged below the brine with a plate, a smaller jar, or another weight. Cover the jar or crock loosely with the lid. Check the corn often over the next 7–10 days, skimming off any white foamy substance that forms on top.

When you are satisfied with the flavor, pour the sour corn into clean glass jars, adding enough brine to submerge the kernels fully. Store the jars, tightly covered, in the refrigerator for up to 6 months.

Melt the butter in a large pan set over low heat. Add the onions and celery and cook, stirring frequently, until they are softened but not browned, about 5 minutes.

Add the potatoes, sour corn, and boiling water to the onion and celery mixture. Season with salt and pepper.

Bring the mixture to a boil, then reduce the heat and simmer until the vegetables are fork-tender, about 10 minutes. Add the smoked trout and cook for another 5 minutes.

Stir in the cream and gently simmer for 1–2 minutes more. Taste and add salt and pepper if needed. Serve hot, garnished with the chives.

Core Sound Clam and Sweet Potato Chowder

Be sure to clean the clams vigorously and thoroughly. Sand and grit is unpleasant even in the best homemade chowder.

Serves 8
....

4 cups water

24 cherrystone (medium) clams, rinsed well and scrubbed clean

1 tablespoon unsalted butter

¼ pound slab bacon or salt pork, diced

2 tablespoons finely chopped garlic

2 medium leeks, tops removed, halved, and cleaned, then sliced into half moons

3 medium sweet potatoes, peeled and cut into medium dice

½ cup dry white wine (such as Pinot Grigio or Sauvignon Blanc)

3 sprigs of fresh thyme

1 bay leaf

2 cups heavy cream

Freshly cracked black pepper

¼ cup chopped fresh parsley

Set a large Dutch oven over medium-high heat, pour in the water, and add the clams. Cover and cook until the clams have opened, 10–15 minutes. *Note*: Discard any clams that fail to open after 15–20 minutes.

Strain the clam broth through a sieve lined with 2 layers of paper towels and set aside. Remove the clam meat from the shells and set aside.

Rinse out the pot, set it on the stove over medium-low heat, and melt the butter. Add the slab bacon or salt pork and cook, stirring occasionally, until the fat has rendered and the pork has started to brown. Remove the pork with a slotted spoon and set aside.

Add the garlic and leeks to the fat and cook, stirring frequently, until the vegetables are soft but not brown, about 10 minutes. Stir in the potatoes and wine and cook until the wine has evaporated and the potatoes have started to soften, about 5 minutes. Add just enough clam broth to cover the potatoes, approximately 3 cups, reserving the rest for another use. Add the thyme and bay leaf. Simmer, partially covered, until the potatoes are tender, about 10 minutes more.

Meanwhile, chop the clams into pieces about the size of the diced pork.

When the potatoes are tender, stir in the cream, chopped clams, and cooked pork. Season with black pepper. Bring the chowder to a simmer and then remove the pot from the heat. Discard the thyme and bay leaf. Allow the chowder to cure for about 10 minutes, reheating it to barely simmering before serving. Portion into deep bowls and garnish with the chopped parsley.

Monkfish Chowder with Sea Beans and Dill

Monkfish is definitely not the most handsome fish in the sea—it's also known as the poor man's lobster—but it absolutely shines in this dish.

Serves 8

....

3 tablespoons unsalted butter

1 large yellow or white onion, roughly chopped

1–2 pounds yellow waxy potatoes, cut into 1-inch chunks

2 quarts of Fish Stock (page 31)

2 pounds monkfish tails

¼ cup sea beans (or thin green beans)

Salt and freshly cracked black pepper to taste

2 egg yolks

½ cup heavy cream

3 tablespoons chopped fresh dill

Melt the butter in a deep, heavy-bottomed pot set over medium heat. Add the onions and cook until translucent but not brown. Add the potatoes and the stock, simmering gently until the potatoes are tender, 15–20 minutes.

Add the monkfish and sea beans, season with salt and pepper, and continue to simmer.

In a medium bowl, whisk the egg yolks with the heavy cream.

Using a ladle in one hand and a whisk in the other, slowly ladle some of the hot soup into the egg and cream mixture while whisking constantly. Repeat this step twice more to temper the eggs and cream. Gently pour the tempered egg and cream mixture into the soup, stirring to combine.

Add the dill and simmer for a few minutes more, but do not boil. Portion the chowder in bowls and serve with good bread and either white wine or a nice beer.

PLEASE DON'T SAY TRASHFISH/UGLYFISH

To clarify, the terms "trashfish" or "uglyfish" are used by food media and organizations outside the seafood industry to describe fish that are less desirable to consumers. These terms aren't regulated or standardized and they vary between fishing regions. So-called trashfish are typically native species that are abundant, sustainable, and readily available at your local fish market; they're just overlooked and underused.

The idea of a marginalized fish is a bit insulting. These are native fish. Just because you don't see them as often on restaurant menus doesn't mean they are inferior. There's a pride to these fish. I've never understood the terms "trashfish" or "uglyfish" anyways. Who wants to eat trash? And how do you measure the ugliness of a fish? How did tilapia become the normal beauty standard for the fish we eat? That must be a cute fish, because we certainly eat a lot of it. These terms just bother me. Is flounder considered pretty? Is salmon prettier than red snapper? For me, these are just native fish and it comes down to how they taste. The flavor is one thing, but there's also texture and oil content, flaky or firm, but none of these qualities correlate with the fish's physical appearance.

I prefer the term "native fish." I was going to name my restaurant Native before I landed on Saltbox, because my ultimate goal was to get my customers to taste and love all these local native fish. There's sure to be a champion of local seafoodways who speaks to the truths of local seafood in your area, too. So if you want to eat as local as possible, find this authority and ask him or her what is good to eat. There's going to be lots you don't know, but you do know what you like.

"Warsh"-Pot Fish Stew

My go-to version of the traditional eastern North Carolina fish stew.

Serves 8

....

½ pound salt pork, cut into medium dice

½ pound semi-dry sausage, cut into 2-inch pieces (I like Mac's
    Air-Dried Country Sausage)

2 pounds (about 6 large) yellow onions, thinly sliced

1 pound (about 1 head) celery, thinly sliced

3 pounds Yukon Gold potatoes, peeled and cut into ½-inch-thick slices

5 pounds fish, cut in 2-inch pieces crossways through the backbone, or
    fillets (rockfish, drum, sheepshead, tripletail, monkfish, dogfish,
    or any other firm fish)

1 cup chopped fresh parsley

Salt and freshly cracked black pepper to taste

2 teaspoons crushed red pepper

2 teaspoons dry yellow mustard

1 tablespoon Worcestershire sauce

2 bay leaves

1 (15-ounce) can diced tomatoes

12 large eggs

Cook the salt pork and sausage in a deep, heavy-bottomed pot set over medium heat until the meat is brown and crispy and the fat has rendered. Remove
the meat and set aside.

Layer the following ingredients in the pot in this order: onions, celery,
potatoes, salt pork and sausage, fish, and parsley, seasoning each layer with
a portion of the salt, black pepper, crushed red pepper, and dry mustard. Top
with the Worcestershire sauce, bay leaves, and tomatoes. Fill the pot with
water to cover the top layer.

Bring the mixture to a boil, then turn the heat to medium low and cook until the fish is tender, about 40 minutes. DO NOT STIR. Give the pot a gentle shake from time to time to keep the stew from sticking.

About 10 minutes before the stew is done, gently crack the eggs into the pot. Cook the eggs in the liquid until the yolks are medium hard. Divide the stew into large bowls, making sure that each bowl gets a good amount of fish, a piece of sausage, a poached egg, and plenty of vegetables.

Core Sound Clams with Gold Tomato and Corn Broth

I got the inspiration for this dish on Shell Island while clamming with my friend Steve Goodwin from Salty Catch (he's a fourth-generation fisherman from Cedar Island). After we dug up the clams, we cooked this dish right there on the beach.

Serves 6
....

4½ pounds fresh North Carolina clams
1 cup dry white wine, such as Pinot Grigio or Sauvignon Blanc
2 tablespoons extra-virgin olive oil, plus more for serving
1 small onion or 2 medium shallots, finely chopped
4 large garlic cloves, finely chopped
¼–½ teaspoon crushed red pepper
1½ cups fresh corn kernels (from about 4 ears)
1½ pounds chopped gold tomatoes (be sure to collect the juice)
1 strip of orange zest
1 teaspoon fresh thyme leaves
Pinch of saffron (optional)
Salt and freshly cracked black pepper to taste
4 tablespoons finely chopped fresh parsley
Lemon wedges, for serving

Rinse the clams in several changes of water and scrub them with a small brush (I like to use a toothbrush). Discard any clams that are open or have cracked shells.

Bring the wine to a boil in a large saucepan, then lower the heat to a simmer and reduce the wine by half. Return the pan to high heat, add the clams, cover, and cook, shaking the pan from time to time until the clams open, 2–3 minutes.

Remove the pan from the heat. Discard any clams that have not opened. Clean the pan and lid and wipe dry.

Set a strainer lined with cheesecloth over a large bowl. Drain the clams and set the liquid and clams aside in separate bowls.

Place the saucepan back over medium heat and add the olive oil. When the oil shimmers, add the onions or shallots and cook, stirring until softened, about 3 minutes. Add the garlic and crushed red pepper and cook for another 30 seconds. Add the corn, tomatoes, orange zest, thyme, saffron, and reserved clam liquid. Bring this mixture to a simmer, reduce the heat to low, and cook, stirring often, until the sauce is slightly reduced and very fragrant, 20–25 minutes. Season with salt and pepper.

Add the clams to the sauce and stir to combine. Add the parsley and stir once more. Ladle portions into wide soup bowls. Top with a drizzle of olive oil and a few drops of freshly squeezed lemon juice.

Cedar Island Fish Pie

I enjoy cooking casserole-style dishes, and pot pies are a favorite meal.
Instead of using a pie dough crust, I like to swap in seasoned mashed potatoes
as the top layer.

Serves 6
....

3 cups whole milk
1 small leek, white part only, chopped
1 small onion, chopped
½ medium celery stalk, chopped
3 large sprigs plus 1 tablespoon chopped fresh parsley, divided
3 whole black peppercorns
1 bay leaf
1½ pounds skinless, boneless white fillets, cut into 2-inch pieces
   (such as monkfish, grouper, dogfish, drum, tilefish, or sturgeon)
½ pound skinless, boneless, hot-smoked white fillets, cut into
   1½-inch pieces
2 pounds russet potatoes, peeled and quartered
¾ cup (1½ sticks) unsalted butter, divided
½ cup heavy cream
Salt and freshly cracked black pepper to taste
Pinch of nutmeg
⅓ cup all-purpose flour
1 teaspoon prepared English mustard (preferably Colman's)
¾ cup grated mild hoop cheddar cheese

In a medium pot set over medium-high heat, bring the milk, leeks, onions,
celery, parsley sprigs, peppercorns, and bay leaf to a boil.

Remove the pot from the heat, cover, and steep for 20 minutes. Strain the
milk, discard the solids, and return the milk to the pot.

Add the fresh and smoked white fish, cover, and bring to a simmer. Continue to simmer over medium heat until the fish is cooked through, 7–8 minutes. Remove the fish to a bowl, cover, and set aside. Reserve the milk.

Bring a large pot of salted water to a boil, add the potatoes, and cook until tender, about 25 minutes. Drain the potatoes, return them to the pot, and set the pot aside, allowing the potatoes to dry out for about 20 minutes. Add 8 tablespoons (1 stick) of the butter, the cream, salt and pepper, and nutmeg, and mash the potatoes until only a few lumps remain. Cover the pot and set aside.

Preheat the oven to 400°.

Melt the remaining butter in a medium pot set over medium heat. Add the flour and stir with a wooden spoon until the butter has absorbed the flour and begins to look dry but not golden, about 4 minutes.

Remove the pot from the heat and gradually pour in the reserved milk, whisking constantly until smooth. Return the pot to the heat, add the mustard and 1 teaspoon of the chopped parsley, and season with salt and pepper. Cook, stirring, until the sauce has thickened, 5–7 minutes.

Pour the sauce into a 3-quart casserole dish. Add the fish and stir to combine. Using a spatula, gently spread the mashed potatoes over the top of the fish mixture, then top with the shredded cheese. Bake until heated through, about 20 minutes. Place the dish under the broiler until the top is golden, 2–3 minutes. Scoop the pie onto plates and garnish with the remaining parsley.

River Camp Fish Muddle

If you're a fan of rockfish stew, you'll enjoy this regional fish dish just as well. Fish muddle varies depending on the cook, but everyone agrees that the most important ingredient is whole fresh fish.

Serves 6

....

FOR THE BROTH

1 (4-pound) whole fish (such as rockfish, drum, or sheepshead)
3 bay leaves
5 sprigs of fresh thyme
1 large yellow onion, peeled and sliced
1 large carrot, peeled and cut into bite-size cubes
1 medium celery stalk with leaves
8 whole black peppercorns
10 drops hot sauce (preferably Texas Pete)
Salt to taste

FOR THE MUDDLE

¼ pound country ham, cut into a small dice
1 tablespoon water
5 scallions, finely chopped
2 large celery stalks, finely diced
2 tablespoons Worcestershire sauce
5 medium russet potatoes, peeled and cut into small dice
Salt and freshly cracked black pepper to taste
¼ cup finely chopped fresh parsley

Prepare the fish. Using a sharp knife, scale and clean the fish and cut off the head, tail, and fins.

Place the fish, its head, and the remaining broth ingredients in a large pot.

Fill the pot with cold water, set it over medium heat, and simmer just until the flesh flakes from the bones. Remove the pot from the heat and cool. Transfer the fish to a plate, pick out all bones, and set the meat aside.

Strain the broth, discard the solids, and return it to the pot. Simmer the broth over high heat until the liquid has reduced to about 1 cup.

Prepare the muddle. Place the ham and water in a large pot set over medium heat. When the ham begins to brown and the fat is translucent, add the scallions and celery and cook until they are moist and soft. Add the Worcestershire sauce, reduced broth, and diced potatoes and simmer until the potatoes are soft, about 15 minutes. Gently stir in the fish and simmer for 10 minutes more. Season with salt and pepper. To serve, ladle the muddle into soup bowls and garnish with the parsley.

North River Camp Clambake

Make sure you follow the steps carefully in this recipe. Use the chicken as your guide to the degree of doneness of everything else in the pot.

Serves 8–10
....

2 quarts Shellfish Stock or water (page 32)

1 cup (2 sticks) unsalted butter

2 (12-ounce) cans lager beer

1 cup apple cider vinegar

4 bay leaves

2 tablespoons crushed red pepper

25–50 cherrystone (medium) clams, rinsed well and scrubbed clean

5 pounds chicken, skinned and cut into large pieces

3 pounds whole sweet potatoes, washed

2 pounds sweet yellow onions, skins removed and cut into eighths

2 pounds celery, cut into 3-inch pieces (about 2 bunches)

6 ears sweet corn, husked, cleaned, and cut into thirds

2 pounds dry link sausage, cut in half

3 pounds large shrimp (21/25 count), shells and heads on

Salt and freshly cracked black pepper to taste

Set a large stockpot over medium heat. Layer the following ingredients in the pot in this order: stock, butter, beer, vinegar, bay leaves, crushed red pepper, clams, chicken, sweet potatoes, onions, and celery. Season with salt and pepper. Cover tightly and simmer for 45–60 minutes.

Add the corn, sausage, and shrimp and simmer, covered, for about 10 minutes more.

Set a colander lined with cheesecloth over a large bowl and drain the broth. Set it aside for dipping. Dump out all the other items onto a table covered with clean cloth or butcher paper and let guests serve themselves.

Stewed Clams and Country Sausage

This dish was inspired by the Spanish Portuguese dish *cataplana*, a long-simmered pork stew with clams. In eastern North Carolina we are known for our pork and our abundant shellfish, so it only made sense to do my version . . . a *cataplana* with Down East sensibilities!

Serves 8
....

50 littleneck (small) clams, rinsed well and scrubbed clean
2 cups dry white wine (Pino Grigio or Sauvignon Blanc), divided
½ cup extra-virgin olive oil
4 tablespoons (½ stick) unsalted butter
2 medium yellow onions, thinly sliced
6 large garlic cloves, thinly sliced
2 teaspoons crushed red pepper
1 pound dry country sausage, cut into ¼-inch-thick slices
2 teaspoons smoked sweet Spanish paprika
Juice of 1 lemon
4 tablespoons chopped fresh parsley
Salt and freshly cracked black pepper to taste
Light rolls

Use a colander lined with paper towels and set over a bowl to strain the clam juice and remove any grit. Reserve the liquid.

In a large skillet, arrange as many clams as will fit in a single layer. Add 1 cup of the white wine and turn the heat to high. Cover the pan and steam the clams until they open. Keep an eye on the pan and check every 1–2 minutes, removing each clam as soon as it pops open. Set aside the opened clams in a bowl. Repeat with the remaining clams.

Tap on the shells of any clams that haven't opened, and sometimes they'll pop. If they stay resolutely closed, discard them.

Wipe the skillet clean and then heat the olive oil and butter over medium-high heat. When the butter has melted, add the onions and sauté until they are soft and the edges have browned a bit. Add the garlic, crushed red pepper, and sausage and cook for another 1–2 minutes.

Sprinkle the paprika over everything. Add the remaining white wine, the clams, and enough of the strained clam juice to cover the ingredients halfway. (If you don't have enough clam juice, add water to make up the difference.) Turn up the heat and boil furiously for about 90 seconds. Turn off the heat, add the lemon juice and chopped herbs, and season with salt and pepper. Portion into deep bowls and serve with light rolls for dipping. Don't forget to put a bowl on the table for the empty clamshells.

Singapore-Style Fish Collar Curry

One of my favorite places to eat fish is Singapore, where one can roam the open-air markets and enjoy the catch of the day, cooked into wonderful bowls of fresh fish curry, at one of the hawker stalls.

A good fish collar curry should taste rich, slightly salty, and a little sour (tangy) and should have the consistency of a thick soup. Do a taste test and season (and spice) the curry to your liking. If you prefer a richer or creamier curry, try adding thick coconut milk instead of thin.

Serves 8
....

20 medium shallots, peeled and cut into chunks
½ large yellow onion, peeled and cut into chunks
1 2½-inch piece of fresh ginger, peeled and cut into chunks
1 small piece of fresh turmeric, peeled and cut into chunks
12 large garlic cloves, peeled
8 tablespoons curry powder
5 tablespoons chili paste (such as sambal oelek), or to taste
¼ cup canola oil, plus more as needed
1 tablespoon salt
2 tablespoons sugar
2 stalks lemongrass (just the bottom third), gently crushed
3 sprigs of curry leaves or 1 large bay leaf
5 cups unsweetened coconut milk
3 tablespoons tamarind paste, mixed with ½ cup water, then strained
1 pound baby eggplants (about 5), cut into 2-inch slices and quartered
1 pound okra, stems removed, cut in half lengthwise
6 plum tomatoes, cut into wedges
4 fish collars (from swordfish, tuna, tilefish, or grouper), skinned and cut in half

In a blender or food processor, pulse the shallots, onions, ginger, turmeric, and garlic into a smooth paste. Add the curry powder and chili paste (the more chili paste, the spicier the dish) and pulse until well combined.

Heat the oil in a large shallow pot set over medium heat. When the oil shimmers, add the curry spice paste and fry gently, stirring continuously to avoid burning. *Note*: If the paste gets a little dry, drizzle in 2–3 tablespoons more oil. Stir in the salt and sugar and cook until the spices become fragrant, about 10 minutes. When the oil floats to the top of the paste and bubbles around the edges, stir in the lemongrass and curry leaves or bay leaf. Cook for another minute. Add the coconut milk and tamarind paste and stir to combine. Increase the heat to medium high and allow the mixture to reach a gentle simmer.

Add the eggplant and simmer for a few minutes. When it start to soften, stir in the okra and tomatoes. Add the fish collars, stirring to coat in the sauce. If the sauce becomes too thick or there is not enough to coat the fish collars, add a little more water. Simmer until the fish collars are cooked through and tender, about 30 minutes. Portion into soup bowls and serve warm.

WHITE BREAD BONE CUSHION

A lot of folks who grew up eating fish choked on the small bones as they ate. This typically happened to the young or to new people eating fish who hadn't been shown how to correctly navigate a fried fish bone, mistaking the small bones for a crispy piece of fried batter. When you were young, the first time you choked and came through it was a rite of passage. But there were a couple of tricks around to help. The first was the act of scoring, which gives fried fish a crispy texture and makes the bones more visible, providing a guide for where to start eating. The second trick was bread or a breadlike item (in my house, it was always sliced white bread). Hot fried fish was often served over a layer of soft white bread to absorb a bit of the fry oil and the juices. If you ever choked, you could grab a piece of this bread and it would act as a kind of cushion to push a stuck bone down your throat. You'd conquer the fish and lose your fear of eating fried seafood.

Perfect Hominy

GRITS AND SEAFOOD

Basic Grits 99

Sweet Potato Grits 100

Shrimp and Grits Fritters 101

Fried Cheddar Grits Cakes 102

Fish and Grits Sticks 103

Grits Dumplings 105

Oyster and Andouille Gravy over Grits 106

Shellfish and Grits Casserole 108

Skillet Speckled Trout with Warm Almond-Caper Vinaigrette and
   Cauliflower "Grits" 109

Crispy Mullet with Roasted Jowls, Creamy Grits, and Fried Sage 111

No matter which part of North Carolina you call home, grits are an essential ingredient of life. Every household and every person reared in North Carolina has had grits at some point. Here I help you earn (and keep) your North Carolina card.

Grits are a simple staple, but they require reverence because they provide for everyone. Grits were and remain an affordable food that can fill many mouths. North Carolinians' love of grits has also fostered a huge industry across the state. Those grits started as fields of corn grown and tended by farmers. Others worked to process the harvested hominy and mill and package the grits. Back in the day, people bought grits by the sack, not in little plastic bags like we do today. Both of my grandmothers bought grits by the pound and used it nearly every day. This is why grits deserve their own chapter, even in a cookbook about seafood.

I realized one day that I instinctively knew how to make grits. I would have been embarrassed to have left my childhood home not knowing how to cook this staple dish. (There's an unspoken rule that if you leave without this knowledge, you'll have to turn in your North Carolina card right away.)

While in the military, I was stationed in Fort Polk, Louisiana. Lots of people there knew about grits, but lots were new to grits, too. In the kitchens, there was a touch of rivalry between regions: Down East versus Low Country versus Creole cooking. Technically, we were supposed to make grits using the military's recipe, with exact specifications for how to feed plenty of hungry soldiers. If we changed anything, we had to mark it in the procedural notes. This was when your homegrown knowledge of grits could shine. Long before *Iron Chef*, there we were, a bunch of military guys waging "Battle Grits" in the morning mess hall.

Everywhere I have traveled, North and South, from the Midwest to the Mid-Atlantic, there's never been a place I've worked or visited that folks didn't know about grits. Even if they didn't eat them regularly, everyone seemed to understand their importance, whether it was from their own heritage or one they adopted in their new home. And I've met many southern and North Carolina transplants who are always happy to talk grits.

At their core, grits are an easy recipe, but just like any easy recipe, people can screw it up. The ratios are defined: one part grits, two parts liquid, a little seasoning, some butter. And the instructions are clear-cut: bring the liquid to a boil; add the grits slowly, stirring to avoid lumps; seasoning and butter come last. The boiling-hot liquid helps the grits bloom, and knowing how to check for the correct degree of doneness is important. Learn these basics and your grits will be perfect every time.

Basic Grits

There is nothing better than a freshly made pot of grits with a big knob of butter melting all over the surface.

Serves 6
....

2 cups water, plus more as needed
2 cups whole milk, plus more as needed
1 cup stone-ground or regular grits
Salt and freshly cracked black pepper to taste
¼ cup heavy cream
2 tablespoons unsalted butter

In a heavy-bottomed saucepan set over medium-low heat, bring the water and milk to a low simmer. While stirring, add the grits. Continue to simmer, stirring often, until the grits are tender to the bite and have the consistency of thick oatmeal. As the grits thicken, stir them more often to keep them from sticking to the pan and scorching. *Note*: Regular grits are done in about 20 minutes, but stone-ground grits require an hour or more to cook (and you may need more milk and water).

Stir in the cream and butter. Season the grits generously with salt and pepper. Remove the pan from the heat and rest the grits, covered, until ready to serve.

Sweet Potato Grits

The sweet and earthy taste of these grits pairs well with grilled and highly spiced seafood.

Serves 6
....

1 recipe Basic Grits (page 100)
¼ cup sour cream
2 tablespoons unsalted butter
1 cup canned sweet potatoes
Salt and freshly cracked black pepper to taste

After making the Basic Grits recipe, remove the pot from the heat and stir in the sour cream and butter. Add the sweet potatoes, stir, and season with salt and pepper.

GRITS, SHRIMP, PORK, AND GRAVY

So, the credit goes to South Carolina for shrimp and grits, obviously, and the dish slowly came up north to our neck of the woods. As it grew in popularity, the essence of the dish was lost with all the bastardized variations. It's a pet peeve of mine and I will argue till the end, shrimp and grits should not be about aesthetics or presentation. I'm not interested in the fancy shrimp tails sitting on top of the grits; they just get in the way. I want all the meat available and no tail. I want to eat everything with a big spoon, and I don't want to pick off inedible pieces with my fingers. In the spirit of stretching the dish, cooks often add too many extras, peppers and this and that. These additions take away from the overall essence of the dish. All that needs to be there is grits (obviously), some sort of pork (salt pork, bacon, country ham, or air-dried sausage), the shrimp, and a thick, saucy gravy. A classic straightforward preparation.

Shrimp and Grits Fritters

This is another take on the traditional shrimp and grits combination. Try dipping them in shellfish gravy and thank me later.

Makes 36 fritters

....

1 recipe Basic Grits (page 100)
2 (5.2-ounce) wheels Boursin herb cheese
½–1 cup shrimp, shelled, deveined, cooked, and chopped
1 cup all-purpose flour
2 cups panko or regular bread crumbs
2 large eggs
1 cup whole milk
1 cup vegetable oil, plus more as needed
Salt and freshly cracked black pepper to taste

Stir in the Boursin cheese and cooked shrimp into the grits and chill for at least 2 hours or overnight.

Put the flour in one shallow bowl and the panko in another. In a third shallow dish, whisk the eggs with the milk.

Shape the shrimp and grits mixture with your hands into walnut-sized 1-ounce balls. Dip the balls into the egg wash, then into the panko, and then into the flour.

In a deep fryer or heavy pot set over medium-high heat, heat the oil until it shimmers.

Fry the grits balls in batches until golden brown, turning the pieces occasionally, 2–3 minutes. Top up the skillet with more oil as necessary. Remove the fritters with a slotted spoon and drain them on paper towels. Season with salt and pepper and serve hot.

Fried Cheddar Grits Cakes

This is my favorite way to use leftover grits.

Serves 6

....

1 recipe Basic Grits (page 100)
1 cup grated white cheddar cheese
3 tablespoons chopped scallions
½ teaspoon finely chopped garlic
Salt and freshly cracked black pepper to taste
½–1 cup vegetable oil, for frying
1¼ cups all-purpose flour
2 large eggs
½ cup whole milk

Grease an 8-inch square baking pan or rimmed baking sheet, line the pan with parchment or wax paper, and grease the top of the paper with nonstick cooking spray. Set aside.

After making the grits, remove the pot from the heat and add the cheese, scallions, and garlic. Season with salt and pepper. Pour the grits onto the prepared baking sheet and smooth them into an even layer with a rubber spatula. Chill the grits until completely firm, at least 1 hour. Using a sharp knife, cut the grits into squares, then keep them chilled until you are ready to fry them.

Heat ½ cup of the oil in a large, heavy skillet or sauté pan to 350°.

Pour the flour into a shallow bowl. In another shallow dish, whisk the eggs with the milk.

Working with one piece at a time, dredge the grits squares in the flour, then dip them into the egg wash and back into the flour.

Fry the squares in batches, turning them occasionally, until they are golden brown, 2–3 minutes. Top up the skillet with more oil as necessary. Remove the grits squares with a slotted spoon and drain them on paper towels. Season with salt and pepper and serve hot.

Fish and Grits Sticks

At some point in time, everyone has enjoyed a Gorton's fisherman fish stick. My version pairs that childhood food memory with a classic eastern North Carolina breakfast tradition.

Serves 6
....

1 recipe Basic Grits (page 100)
3 cups hot-smoked trout (I prefer the hot-smoked trout from
    Sunburst Trout Farm)
1 cup poached flounder fillet, skin removed
½ cup thinly sliced fresh chives
½ teaspoon freshly cracked black pepper, plus more to taste
1½ cups all-purpose flour
2 large eggs
¼ cup water
3 cups panko or regular bread crumbs
Vegetable oil, for frying

Lightly grease a 9-inch-square baking pan with nonstick cooking spray and set aside.

After making the grits, remove the pot from the heat and let stand for 5 minutes. Mix in the trout, flounder, chives, and pepper. Spoon the mixture into the baking pan and chill for at least 4 hours or overnight.

Gently invert the chilled grits onto a large cutting board. Cut the grits into ¾-inch wide, 4-inch-long strips.

Pour the flour into a shallow bowl. In another shallow dish, whisk together the eggs and water. Place the panko in a third shallow dish.

Working with one piece at a time, dredge the grits-fish pieces in the flour, dip them in the egg wash, and roll them in the panko, pressing gently to adhere. Place the pieces on a sheet pan and set it in the freezer for 15 minutes.

Fill a large, heavy skillet with 1 inch of oil and heat the oil to 350°.

Working in batches, fry the sticks, turning them occasionally, until they are golden brown, 3–4 minutes. Remove the sticks with a slotted spoon and drain them on paper towels. Top up the skillet with more oil as needed. Repeat with the remaining sticks. Season with salt and pepper and serve hot.

Grits Dumplings

The inspiration for this recipe comes from my love of matzo ball soup.
When I make Hatteras clam chowder, I use this recipe instead of the traditional
cornmeal dumplings, creating what I like to call . . . GRITZO BALL SOUP!

Makes 9 medium dumplings
....

¾ cup uncooked quick-cooking grits
½ cup all-purpose flour
1 tablespoon grated yellow onion
1½ teaspoons baking powder
2 teaspoons chicken bouillon
½ cup whole milk
3 tablespoons unsalted butter, softened
Salt and freshly cracked black pepper to taste

In a heatproof bowl, combine the grits, flour, onions, baking powder, and bouillon.

In a small saucepan set over high heat, bring the milk and butter to a boil, stirring occasionally. Pour the hot milk over the grits and stir to combine. Let stand for 5 minutes.

Bring a large pot with ½ inch water to a boil over medium-high heat. Coat a steamer basket with nonstick cooking spray.

Shape the grits mixture into 9 balls (about 2 tablespoons each). Place the balls in the prepared steamer basket and gently lower it into the pot of boiling water, making sure that the bottom of the basket does not touch the water. Cover and cook until the dumplings are puffy and slightly firm to the touch, about 15 minutes.

Transfer the dumplings to serving bowls. If they stick together, gently pull or cut them apart. To serve, pour warm broth or soup over the dumplings in bowls. *Note*: The dumplings will expand in the broth.

Oyster and Andouille Gravy over Grits

Shellfish and pork have an affinity for each other, especially when paired in this hearty, sweater-weather meal that's perfect for the North Carolina oyster season. The secret to this and many other flavorful dishes is browned flour. When the weather gets cold, set aside half an hour to prepare a batch of this simple but oh-so-necessary ingredient to thicken and flavor rich-tasting dishes all season long.

Serves 8

....

1½ cups all-purpose flour

3 tablespoons unsalted butter

6 ounces andouille sausage, diced

2 teaspoons vegetable oil

1 cup diced sweet onion

1 cup sliced okra

½ cup diced green bell pepper

2 large garlic cloves, finely chopped

1½ teaspoons "Joint" Seasoning (page 33)

1 cup clam juice (bottled is okay)

1 (15-ounce) can diced tomatoes

1 pound freshly shucked oysters

Preheat the oven to 400°.

In a 12-inch cast-iron skillet, spread the flour in an even layer. Bake until the flour is the color of pecan shells, 20–25 minutes, stirring with a wooden spoon every 7 minutes. Remove the flour from the skillet and cool completely. Reserve 3 tablespoons and set aside; refrigerate the rest in an airtight container for another use for up to 2 months.

Melt the butter in a large skillet set over medium heat and cook the sausage until lightly browned. Add the oil, onions, okra, bell peppers, garlic, and Saltbox Seasoning and sauté until the vegetables are tender, about 3 minutes. Sprinkle the reserved browned flour over the sausage mixture and stir to combine. Stir in the clam juice and increase the heat to medium high. Bring the mixture to a boil and add the tomatoes, stirring occasionally, until the gravy thickens, about 3 minutes. Add the oysters and cook until the oysters are firm, about 5 minutes. Serve hot over Basic Grits (page 100).

Shellfish and Grits Casserole

Prepare this dish for any festive event. Put it in your heirloom casserole cookware, and it will definitely be a showstopper.

Serves 6

....

3 large eggs, lightly beaten
½ cup (1 stick) unsalted butter, melted
1 medium green bell pepper, diced
2 teaspoons garlic powder
1 teaspoon Old Bay Seasoning
1 teaspoon hot sauce (preferably Texas Pete)
½ cup finely chopped fresh parsley
1 cup fine bread crumbs
1 cup chopped scallions
½ cup grated Parmesan cheese
1 recipe Basic Grits (page 100)
5 ounces medium shrimp (51/60 count), peeled and deveined
5 ounces lump crabmeat
5 ounces shucked oysters

Preheat the oven to 325°. Lightly grease a 11 × 7-inch baking dish with non-stick cooking spray and set aside.

In a large bowl, combine the eggs, butter, bell peppers, garlic powder, Old Bay, hot sauce, parsley, bread crumbs, scallions, and Parmesan.

Gradually stir about one-fourth of the hot grits into the egg mixture to temper the eggs. Add the rest of the grits, stirring constantly. Fold in the shellfish and combine thoroughly.

Pour the mixture into the baking dish and bake until set, about 1 hour. Let stand for 10 minutes, then portion onto plates.

Skillet Speckled Trout with Warm Almond-Caper Vinaigrette and Cauliflower "Grits"

You can eat this play on traditional breakfast fish and grits at any time of day. Cauliflower pulsed in a food processor looks just like large-grain hominy and makes a wonderful bowl of "grits."

Serves 4

....

FOR THE CAULIFLOWER "GRITS"

2 tablespoons unsalted butter or coconut oil

1 medium yellow onion, finely chopped

1 large head cheddar or orange cauliflower, cut into florets

1 cup vegetable broth

1 cup whole milk

¼ cup Boursin herb cheese

Salt and freshly cracked black pepper to taste

FOR THE FISH

¼ cup chopped flat-leaf parsley

¼ cup toasted sliced almonds

2 tablespoons extra-virgin olive oil, divided

1 tablespoon grated lemon zest

1½ tablespoons fresh lemon juice

1 tablespoon drained and chopped capers

4 (6-ounce) trout fillets

½ teaspoon salt

½ teaspoon freshly cracked black pepper

To make the grits, pulse the cauliflower florets in a food processor until they are the consistency of rice. Alternatively, finely chop the florets with a sharp knife.

Melt the butter or coconut oil in a large saucepot set over medium heat. Add the onions and cook until they soften. Add the cauliflower, broth, and milk. Bring the mixture to a boil, then lower the heat and cover. Simmer until the liquid is mostly absorbed, about 10 minutes. Stir in the cheese and season with salt and pepper. Cover and set aside on the warm stove while you prepare the fish.

In a small bowl, combine the parsley, almonds, 1 tablespoon of the oil, lemon zest, lemon juice, and capers. Set aside.

Rinse the fillets under cold water and pat them dry with paper towels. Season both sides with the salt and pepper.

Set a large cast-iron skillet over medium-high heat. Pour the remaining oil in the skillet and swirl to coat the pan. Arrange the fillets in the pan skin-side down and cook for about 5 minutes. Flip the fish and cook until the flesh flakes easily when tested with a fork, 1–2 minutes. Remove the fish from the skillet and set aside.

Put the parsley mixture in the skillet and cook for 30 seconds, stirring constantly.

To serve, portion the cauliflower grits into bowls and top with a fillet. Spoon the hot parsley mixture over the top.

NO SUCH THING AS NORTH CAROLINA DINNER GRITS

Grits can get very technical here in North Carolina. Technically, you can have grits any time of the day and people will argue about the differences in preparation and proper time for serving. Back home, we have fish and grits, which is technically a breakfast dish and has always been served with bacon or ham. In my house, it was served as an occasional lunch offering, if there were leftover breakfast grits that needed to be used up, but we never had fish and grits for dinner. And to get even more technical, you can talk about the types of grits. There were two (at least at my Piggly Wiggly): white Quaker brand grits with the old white man on the label and yellow. I grew up with white grits, instant, one-hour. We never used the yellow.

Crispy Mullet with Roasted Jowls, Creamy Grits, and Fried Sage

This is my personal version of fish and grits. I like the meatiness of pork jowls—they remind me of a southern brunch plate—but you can use bacon or country sausage if you prefer.

Serves 4

....

FOR THE GRITS

3 cups chicken broth, plus more
   as needed
1 cup heavy cream
1 cup water
½ cup (1 stick) unsalted butter
1 teaspoon freshly cracked
black pepper

1 teaspoon garlic powder
1 teaspoon onion powder
1 cup sharp cheddar cheese,
   grated
Hot sauce to taste (preferably
   Texas Pete)

FOR THE FISH

4 ounces pork jowls, sliced
4–6 mullet fillets
2 teaspoons freshly cracked
   black pepper
1 teaspoon garlic powder
1 teaspoon onion powder
1 cup stone-ground or
   regular grits

1 teaspoon sweet paprika
1 large egg, beaten
2 tablespoons hot sauce
   (preferably Texas Pete)
1 tablespoon yellow mustard
2 cups fine yellow corn flour
Vegetable oil, for frying
1 small bunch of fresh sage leaves

To make the grits, combine the chicken broth, cream, and water in a large stockpot set over high heat. Once heated through, add the butter, pepper, and garlic and onion powders. Bring to a boil and slowly stir in the grits, whisking continuously to prevent lumps. Reduce the heat to low, cover, and cook until the grits are tender, stirring occasionally, for about 30 minutes.

While the grits are cooking, set a pan over medium-high heat and brown the sliced jowls until crispy. Remove the jowls and drain them on paper towels.

Check the grits, adding broth to thin the mixture if needed. Whisk in the cheese and hot sauce, cover, and set aside.

Rinse the fish fillets in cold water and pat them dry with paper towels. Cut the fish into ½-inch strips and place the strips in a large shallow bowl.

In a small bowl, mix together the pepper, garlic and onion powders, and paprika. Divide the seasonings in half. In another small bowl, whisk together the egg, hot sauce, and mustard.

Lightly toss the fish with half of the seasonings. Pour the egg mixture over the seasoned fish and gently toss to coat.

Place the corn flour in a brown paper bag or plastic freezer bag, add the remaining seasonings, and shake to combine. Add the fish to the bag and gently shake to coat.

Fill a large Dutch oven with 3–4 inches of oil and heat the oil to 350°.

Remove a few pieces of fish from the bag, gently tapping to remove excess flour. Carefully add the fish to the oil and fry until they are golden brown and flaky to the touch, 7–8 minutes. Remove the fish and drain on paper towels. Continue with the remaining fish.

Fry the sage leaves in the oil remaining in the pan for just a few seconds until they curl and crisp up. Drain the fried leaves on paper towels.

To serve, spoon a portion of grits into a bowl, place a few pieces of fish on top, and garnish with the jowls and sage.

The Spread

HOT AND COLD SIDES

Saltbox Bread and Butter Vegetable Slaw **115**

Skillet-Fried Broccoli **117**

Hush-Honeys® **118**

Long-Simmered Green Beans **120**

Country Fried Potatoes with Onions and Green Peppers **121**

Skillet Succotash **122**

Oven-Stewed Tomatoes **124**

Crispy Brussels Sprouts with Garlic and Lemon **125**

Cucumber, Onion, and Herb Salad **126**

Lemon Rice **128**

Saltbox Seafood Joint meals are rounded out by side dishes. And one of the most beloved of my sides are my Hush-Honeys. Before we get to all the delicious recipes that make the plate, I want to tell you about the origins of Hush-Honeys.

Back in high school, I used to grab lunch at a restaurant in New Bern called Friday's 1890. You could get a dozen hushpuppies for fifty cents or so. The dough had onion and seasoning, and the hushpuppies were cranked out in a donut hopper that had a die at the bottom to give them their traditional crescent shape. For me, these were proper hushpuppies, because the staff made them to order and they came out hot and fresh in a bag along with a little packet of butter—the perfect cheap lunch. This is how I measure all other hushpuppies. Some people tend to overthink the recipe, and others let the oil get too hot. Sometimes the batter is too dense for the fryer: when the inside isn't cooked and the outside is all dark, that just offends me.

When I opened Saltbox, I wanted to set my food apart from every other seafood concept. I was always thinking, "What can I do better every day?" Initially, I didn't offer any cornmeal-based fried items, but I quickly realized that hushpuppies were SOP (standard operating procedure) in North Carolina and I had to put them on the menu. I went back to all my hushpuppy experiences, remembering where they went right or wrong or were just too fancy (such as when people put honey in the butter). I started thinking about the first Italian restaurants I worked in after culinary school, where I made a lightly fried dessert called *zeppole*, which we'd coat in a sweet glaze. I wanted to add some heat and some spice, too. Saltbox needed a hook dish, one you couldn't get any other place. That's how the Saltbox Seafood Joint Hush-Honeys came to be.

Hush-Honeys are made in the traditional crescent or football shape associated with eastern North Carolina. We make our dough about twenty-four hours in advance before we send it through a hopper that is positioned over hot oil, ready for when an order comes through. The Hush-Honeys even have their own specific bowl in which the little pieces get tossed in seasoning before being put into paper trays and topped with a honey glaze.

At first, I had a hard time with people saying "hushpuppy," so we just gently corrected people when they ordered. I promoted Hush-Honeys in the spirit of Mohammed Ali, who said he was the greatest and so overwhelmed his foes with his confidence. I spoke to the goodness of Hush-Honeys, and people listened. I make all my side dishes with this same confidence.

Saltbox Bread and Butter Vegetable Slaw

In the spirit of homemade bread and butter pickles, time is the key to this slaw. The longer it sits, the more the sweet, sour, and tangy notes will develop.

Serves 6
....

¼ cup apple cider vinegar
1 tablespoon orange juice concentrate
1 tablespoon Dijon mustard
1 tablespoon honey or 1 teaspoon of sugar
¼ cup extra-virgin olive oil
½ head of green cabbage (use the dark green leaves), thinly sliced
1 cup thinly sliced radicchio (or red cabbage)
2 large carrots, peeled and shredded
3 scallions, thinly sliced
¼ cup chopped fresh parsley
Salt and freshly cracked black pepper to taste

In a small bowl, whisk together the vinegar, orange juice, mustard, honey or sugar, and olive oil. Set aside.

In a large bowl, combine the shredded cabbages, carrots, scallions, and parsley.

Pour a small amount of the vinegar dressing over the slaw and mix. Add more dressing to taste and season with salt and pepper. Refrigerate for at least 24 hours before serving.

WEST INDIES SALAD MYTHOLOGY

West Indies salad is a side dish that comes from a family restaurant known for seafood out of lower Mobile, Alabama. Supposedly, the father was a merchant marine and spent some time down in the islands. When he was stationed there, he would take spiny lobster meat and marinate it in vinegar and mix it together with his favorite cold side, cucumber and onion salad. Back at the restaurant in Mobile, he had an abundance of crab meat and needed something to serve to people as an appetizer while they waited. So, he remade his island salad with crab meat, onions, apple cider vinegar, and vegetable oil. It would marinate and chill overnight, and the next day it was served with saltines and went out to every table. I like this story and I like to use North Carolina crab (first and foremost) and elevate things with some finely chopped shallots, fresh parsley, champagne vinegar, and a mild olive oil. For a final Saltbox touch, I toast my saltines with Old Bay Seasoning.

Skillet-Fried Broccoli

**The more you brown and caramelize broccoli, the sweeter it will taste.
This recipe allows all the natural sugars and moisture in broccoli to shine.**

Serves 6

....

2 pounds broccoli
2 tablespoons bacon grease
1 teaspoon finely chopped garlic
½ teaspoon crushed red pepper
2 tablespoons grated lemon zest
1 teaspoon ground coriander
Salt to taste

Rinse and pat dry the broccoli. Cut it into large florets.

Melt the bacon grease in a large skillet set over medium-high heat. Add the broccoli florets and fry them until they are brown and crisp on all sides, 5–7 minutes.

Remove the skillet from the heat and stir in the garlic and crushed red pepper, tossing to coat the broccoli. Season with the lemon zest, coriander, and salt. Serve hot.

Hush-Honeys®

The idea for this dish comes from my love of North Carolina–style hushpuppies
and the Italian fried-dough dessert *zeppole*. That love turned into Hush-Honeys.
Folks come from near and far just for a tray of these sweet, hot treats.

Serves 8

....

1 tablespoon ground fennel, toasted

1 tablespoon ground coriander, toasted

1 tablespoon dried ground lemon peel or freshly grated lemon zest

1 tablespoon plus 2 teaspoons salt, divided

2 cups fine polenta (or fine cornmeal)

1 cup "00" flour (preferably Caputo) or ½ cup all-purpose flour
    plus ½ cup fine cornmeal

2 tablespoons sugar

4 teaspoons baking powder

1 cup sour cream

¼ cup canned or frozen creamed corn

¼ teaspoon hot sauce (preferably Texas Pete)

1 medium yellow onion, grated

Canola oil, for frying

8 tablespoons honey

In a small bowl, combine the fennel, coriander, lemon peel or zest, and 2 teaspoons of the salt. Set aside.

In a large bowl, combine the polenta, flour (or flour and cornmeal), sugar, baking powder, and the remaining salt. In a separate bowl, whisk together the sour cream, creamed corn, hot sauce, and onions. Combine the creamy mixture with the dry ingredients and let sit for 10 minutes.

Fill a 6-quart Dutch oven with 2 inches of oil and heat the oil to 375°.

Transfer the rested batter to a piping bag fitted with a ¾-inch diameter round tip (a zip-top bag with a snipped corner works well in a pinch). Keep a pair of scissors nearby.

Working in batches, pipe and cut 3-inch logs of batter into the hot oil. Fry the pieces until golden brown, 1–2 minutes. Remove the pieces with a slotted spoon and drain them on paper towels. Repeat with the remaining batter.

Toss the fried pieces with the fennel spice mixture, drizzle with honey, and serve hot.

Long-Simmered Green Beans

These green beans, cooked low and slow until soft and tender in a bacon-infused broth, are a far cry from those canned beans that sit in cafeteria steam trays all day.

Serves 6
....

7 thick bacon slices, cut crosswise into thin strips
1 cup thinly sliced yellow onions
2 pounds fresh green beans, trimmed and longer beans snapped in half
2 cups chicken broth
2 cups water
1 teaspoon salt, plus more to taste
½ teaspoon freshly cracked black pepper, plus more to taste
½ teaspoon garlic powder
¼ teaspoon crushed red pepper
1 bay leaf
1 tablespoon unsalted butter

Cook the bacon in a large pot until the strips are brown and crisp and the fat has rendered. Remove the bacon strips and set aside.

Cook the onions in the bacon fat until they are soft, then add the green beans and all the remaining ingredients except the butter. Bring the mixture to a boil, turn the heat to medium low, cover, and simmer for 1–2 hours, stirring occasionally.

The goal is to create a "pot liquor" with all the flavors and seasonings of the beans and spices. Continue to cook until the pot liquor reduces to intensify the flavor.

When the beans are very tender, add the butter and bacon and stir to combine. Check the beans for seasoning, adding salt and pepper as needed. Serve warm.

Country Fried Potatoes
with Onions and Green Peppers

If home fries and potato chips had a baby, this would be it.

Serves 8
....

7 Idaho russet potatoes, peeled and cut crosswise into ¼-inch-thick slices
Canola oil, for frying
2 tablespoons extra-virgin olive oil
1 small green bell pepper, stemmed, seeded, and thinly sliced
2 small yellow onions, thinly sliced
2 large garlic cloves, finely chopped
1 tablespoon ground coriander, toasted
1 tablespoon ground fennel, toasted
2 tablespoons finely chopped fresh parsley
1 tablespoon grated lemon zest
Salt and freshly cracked black pepper to taste

Bring a large pot of salted water to a boil, add the potato slices, and cook until just tender, 5–8 minutes. Drain the potatoes and spread them on paper towels to dry.

Fill a 6-quart saucepan with 2 inches of canola oil and heat the oil to 375°. Working in batches, deep-fry the potatoes until they are crisp, about 7 minutes. Remove the potatoes with a slotted spoon and drain them on paper towels.

Heat the olive oil in a sauté pan over medium heat. When the oil shimmers, add the bell peppers and cook for 2 minutes. Add the onions and garlic and sauté until the onions are slightly caramelized but not too dark, about 2 minutes more. Remove the pan from the heat and stir in the coriander and fennel. Add the fried potatoes and toss with the vegetables. Add the parsley and lemon zest and toss once more. Season with salt and pepper and serve hot.

Skillet Succotash

For this southern classic, I like to swap lima beans for crowder or purple hull peas. It gives the dish more character and a hint of heirloom flavor.

Serves 6

....

2 cups fresh crowder or purple hull peas
½ small yellow onion
4 sprigs of fresh thyme
1 large garlic clove
3 thick bacon slices
1 medium sweet onion, chopped
2 cups fresh corn kernels (from about 6 ears)
1 pint cherry tomatoes, halved
1 cup canned white hominy, drained
2 tablespoons unsalted butter
1 tablespoon red wine vinegar
1½ tablespoons chopped fresh dill
1½ tablespoons chopped fresh chives
Salt and freshly cracked black pepper to taste

Bring a large saucepan of water to a boil over medium-high heat. Add the peas, onions, thyme, and garlic. Reduce the heat to medium and simmer, stirring occasionally, until the peas are tender, about 20 minutes. Drain the peas and reserve ¾ cup of the cooking liquid. Discard the onions, thyme, and garlic.

In a large skillet set over medium heat, cook the bacon until crisp, turning once. Remove the bacon and drain the slices on paper towels. Reserve 2 tablespoons of the rendered fat. Crumble the bacon once it has cooled.

Set the same skillet with the reserved bacon fat over medium-high heat, add the onions, and sauté for 5 minutes. Add the corn and cook, stirring often, until the kernels are tender, about 6 minutes. Stir in the tomatoes, hominy, and reserved cooking liquid. Continue to cook, stirring occasionally, for 5 minutes more. Add the butter, vinegar, dill, and chives and stir to combine. Sprinkle with the crumbled bacon and season with salt and pepper.

Oven-Stewed Tomatoes

These stewed tomatoes are excellent by themselves, but they are even better served over creamy salted grits or rice.

Serves 8

. . . .

2 (28-ounce) cans whole peeled tomatoes
3 stale white sandwich bread slices, crusts removed
2 tablespoons unsalted butter, melted
3 tablespoons light brown sugar
½ teaspoon coarse salt, plus more to taste
⅛ teaspoon freshly cracked pepper, plus more to taste

Preheat the oven to 350°.

Using a wire-mesh strainer, strain 1 can of tomatoes and reserve the liquid for another use. Pour the strained tomatoes into a 2-quart ovenproof casserole dish. Add the second can of tomatoes, including the juice. Crush the tomatoes into large chunks with your fingers. Roughly tear the bread slices into pieces and add them to the tomatoes. Stir in the butter, brown sugar, salt, and pepper.

Cover the casserole and bake until the tomatoes are tender, about 45 minutes. Season with additional salt and pepper, if desired, and serve warm.

Crispy Brussels Sprouts with Garlic and Lemon

As a kid I enjoyed skillet-fried cabbage, so it was only natural for me to take the concept and apply it to brussels sprouts.

Serves 8

. . . .

1 large garlic clove, crushed, finely chopped, and mashed into a paste
¼ teaspoon salt
⅛ teaspoon cayenne pepper
1½ tablespoons lemon juice
1 tablespoon extra-virgin olive oil
Canola or peanut oil, for frying
2 pounds brussels sprouts, rinsed, patted dry, trimmed, and
    cut in half lengthwise
"Joint" Seasoning (page 33) to taste
Salt to taste

In a small bowl, whisk together the garlic, salt, cayenne, lemon juice, and olive oil. Set aside.

Fill a deep fryer or deep, heavy-bottomed skillet with 2 inches of canola or peanut oil and heat the oil to 375°.

Place the brussels sprouts in a wire basket and gently lower it into the oil. Immediately cover the pan to prevent the hot oil from splattering on you or your countertop (the sprouts have a high moisture content and will splatter during the first minute of cooking). Fry the sprouts until they are golden brown, 4–5 minutes. Remove the sprouts and drain them on paper towels.

Place the fried sprouts in a large bowl, drizzle with the garlic-lemon dressing, and toss until well coated. Sprinkle with "Joint" Seasoning and salt and serve piping hot.

Cucumber, Onion, and Herb Salad

Cool and always tasty. The key to a good cucumber salad is the thickness of the slices and the ratio of dressing to vegetable. Make sure the cucumbers are submerged in the dressing, and allow the dish to marinate so that the flavors come together.

Serves 8
....

2 large English cucumbers
1 medium white onion
Salt to taste
3 tablespoons extra-virgin olive oil
Juice of ½ lemon
3 tablespoons distilled white vinegar
1 tablespoon honey
1 teaspoon Dijon mustard
2 tablespoons chopped fresh dill
2 tablespoons chopped fresh parsley
1 tablespoon chopped fresh mint
¼ teaspoon garlic powder
Pinch of crushed red pepper

Using a sharp knife or a mandolin, thinly slice the cucumbers and onions. Place the slices in a bowl and sprinkle them with salt.

In another bowl, combine the remaining ingredients to make the dressing.

Toss the dressing with the cucumbers, then chill for 30 minutes. Season with salt, and serve immediately.

CHURCH SPREADS AND CUCUMBER AND ONION SALAD

The church was always most populated when there was food. The women of the church did a lot of the cooking—all the cooking, frankly—and used the term "spread" because you spread the whole table with the dishes people brought to share. A lot of times, it was more vegetables and side dishes than anything else, but there was also chicken, some sort of pork dish, and usually a little transportable fryer for last-minute fry-ups. Everybody seemed to have a garden and pulled stuff out of it and did simple things with what they harvested. Traditional things like coleslaw, some sort of potato preparation (often boiled white potatoes, peeled, and cooked in seasoned liquid, which made the potatoes soft and very popular), Brunswick stew, tomato salad with mayo and bacon, green beans that had been cooked for a very long time, and cucumber and onion salad. Everybody grew cucumbers and this salad was simple, not too impressive, but everybody loved it. Vinegar, salt, pepper, onions sliced really thin, and a little clear, white salad oil (which today we'd call vegetable oil) dressing (definitely not a vinaigrette). Iced and chilled and so straightforward. And it just makes sense to pair with fish.

Lemon Rice

The Carolinas have a long history with rice, but over the years I have become a big fan of basmati rice because of its aromatic qualities. I know that we all enjoy our traditional accompaniments with fried seafood, but try this recipe and you'll be surprised how well it goes with the meal.

Serves 8
....

2 tablespoons extra-virgin olive oil

½ chopped yellow onion

1½ cups basmati rice, rinsed well and drained

3 large garlic cloves, finely chopped

2 teaspoons grated lemon zest

2 cups chicken stock

½ cup water

¼ cup fresh lemon juice, plus more to taste

¾ teaspoon salt, plus more to taste

2 tablespoons freshly chopped parsley

2 tablespoons freshly chopped chives

¼ teaspoon ground turmeric

½ teaspoon ground fennel

2 tablespoons unsalted butter

Freshly cracked black pepper to taste

¼ cup crumbled feta cheese

Heat the oil in a large saucepan over medium-high heat. When the oil shimmers, add the onions and sauté until soft, about 5 minutes. Add the rice, garlic, and lemon zest and sauté for another minute. Stir in the chicken stock, water, lemon juice, and all the seasonings. Bring the rice to a boil, then reduce the heat to low, cover, and cook until the water has evaporated and the rice is tender, stirring once about halfway through, 12–15 minutes. *Note*: If the liquid evaporates but your rice is still quite undercooked (keeping in mind that it will steam for 10 minutes after being removed from the heat), add a little more liquid and continue to cook until tender.

Once the water has evaporated, remove the pan from the heat, stir, cover, and let sit for 10 minutes. Stir in the butter. Taste and add more lemon juice, salt, and pepper, if desired. Sprinkle with the crumbled feta and fluff with a fork. Serve hot.

Menus

The Saltbox Menu

This has been the fundamental menu since I first opened Saltbox in 2012.

Fried or grilled in-season fish
Saltbox Bread and Butter Vegetable Slaw (page 115)
Hush-Honeys (page 118)
Country Fried Potatoes with Onions and Green Peppers (page 121)
Cocktail Sauce (page 36) and Tartar Sauce (page 37)
Skillet-Fried Broccoli (page 117)

Seabreeze Fish Fry

This menu is a reference to the historical Seabreeze community in Wilmington, North Carolina, where African Americans used to go for summertime vacations.

Fried whole spot and croaker (page 49)
Boiled potatoes
Oven-Stewed Tomatoes (page 124)
Hush-Honeys (page 118)
Pickled shrimp
Fried Chicken

Beach Cookout

Going to the beach and building a fire to cook local seafood is the classic North Carolina summertime activity.

Hickory Charcoal Mullet with BBQ Butter (page 68)
Grilled or Broiled Oysters with Carolina Treet Butter (page 64)
Saltbox Bread and Butter Vegetable Slaw (page 115)
Cucumber, Onion, and Herb Salad (page 126)
Foil-baked sweet potatoes

Picnic Season

Gather this together and spend some time with your family on a nice, slow Sunday.

Potted crab
Pickled shrimp
West Indies salad (page 116)
Crackers
Cocktail Sauce (page 36) and Cold Mustard-Herb Sauce (page 38)

Fall Gathering

Coastal sweater-weather eats.

River Camp Fish Muddle (page 89)
Fried Cheddar Grits Cakes (page 102)
Collard greens
Hush-Honeys (page 118)
Lemon Rice (page 128)

Line Drawing Credits

amberjack	Wikimedia Commons
bluefish	John Norton
butterfish	Muir Way
catfish	John Norton
clams	John Norton
conch	antiqueimgnet/iStockphoto.com
crab	John Norton
croaker	John Norton
dogfish	Muir Way
flounder	John Norton
grouper	John Norton
hogfish	ThePalmer/iStockphoto.com
lionfish	John Norton
mackeral	John Norton
monkfish	Hein Nouwens/Shutterstock.com
mullet	John Norton
oysters	John Norton
porgy	John Norton
ribbonfish	Valery Evlakhov/Shutterstock.com
rockfish	John Norton
scallops	John Norton
sheepshead	ThePalmer/iStockphoto.com
shrimp	John Norton
snapper	John Norton
spot	John Norton
sugar toad	Wikimedia Commons
swordfish	John Norton
tripletail	Wikimedia Commons
trout	John Norton
tuna	John Norton
white/yellow perch	benoitb/iStockphoto.com
whiting/sea mullet	John Norton

Index

Italic page numbers refer to photographs, illustrations, and charts.

A

African American chefs, 6, 17

Agraria (Washington, D.C.), 7

Ali, Mohammed, 114

All-Purpose (AP) Seafood Dredge, 40

almonds: Skillet Speckled Trout with Warm Almond-Caper Vinaigrette and Cauliflower "Grits," 109–10

amberjack

    cuts of, 26

    Griddled Amberjack Collars with Fresh Thyme, 66

    as loin fish, 24

    seasonality, 27

andouille sausage: Oyster and Andouille Gravy over Grits, 106–7

apple cider vinegar: Smoked Mullet with Cider-Sorghum Syrup Glaze, 70–71

B

Basic Grits, 99

Basie, Count, 46

bay leaf: Broiled Green-Tail Shrimp with Bay Leaf Butter, 61

Bayless, Rick, 7

Beach Cookout menu, 131

bluefish

    Ritz Cracker–Crusted Bluefish Cakes, 43–44

    as round fish, 20

    seasonality, 27

    Smoky Deviled Bluefish, 67

Bop City. *See* Freeman's Beach/Seabreeze

Broccoli, Skillet-Fried, 117, 130

Broiled Green-Tail Shrimp with Bay Leaf Butter, 61

Broiled Panko-and-Herb-Crusted Triggerfish, 63

Brown, James, 46

brussels sprouts: Crispy Brussels Sprouts with Garlic and Lemon, 125

butter

    Broiled Green-Tail Shrimp with Bay Leaf Butter, 61

    Grilled or Broiled Oysters with Carolina Treet Butter, 64, 131

    Hickory Charcoal Mullet with BBQ Butter, 68, 131

butterfish (harvestfish)

    cuts of, 25

    as flatfish, 22

    seasonality, 27

butterflied cut, 25

C

"calabash," definition of, 48

Calabash, North Carolina, 48

capers: Skillet Speckled Trout with Warm Almond-Caper Vinaigrette and Cauliflower "Grits," 109–10

Carolina Treet Cooking Barbecue Sauce: Grilled or Broiled Oysters with Carolina Treet Butter, 64, 131

casseroles
Cedar Island Fish Pie, 87–88
Oven-Stewed Tomatoes, 124
Shellfish and Grits Casserole, 108

cataplana, 92

catfish
cuts of, 25
as round fish, 20
seasonality, 27

cauliflower: Skillet Speckled Trout with Warm Almond-Caper Vinaigrette and Cauliflower "Grits," 109–10

Cedar Island Fish Pie, 87–88

Chapel Hill, North Carolina, 13

charcoaling seafood. *See* grilling, smoking, and charcoaling seafood

cheddar cheese: Fried Cheddar Grits Cakes, 102, 131

Chicago, Illinois, 6–7

Chicken-Fried Sugar Toads, 55

Chitlin Circuit, 46

chowders
about, 75–76
Core Sound Clam and Sweet Potato Chowder, 79–80
Hot-Smoked Trout and Sour Corn Chowda, 77–78
Monkfish Chowder with Sea Beans and Dill, 81

church spreads, and cucumber and onion salad, 127

clambakes, 62

clams
Core Sound Clam and Sweet Potato Chowder, 79–80
Core Sound Clams with Gold Tomato and Corn Broth, 85–86
North River Camp Clambake, 91
seasonality, 27, 62
as shellfish, 23
shucked, 26
Stewed Clams and Country Sausage, 15, 92–93

Clark, Patrick, 6, 7

cleaning crab, 42

cleaning fish, 25

Cocktail Sauce, 36, 130, 131

Cold Mustard-Herb Sauce, 38, 131

collar cut, 26

conch
seasonality, 27
as shellfish, 23
shucked, 26

cooking oil, fish grease, 40

Core Sound Clam and Sweet Potato Chowder, 79–80

Core Sound Clams with Gold Tomato and Corn Broth, 85–86

Core Sound Waterfowl Museum, Harkers Island, 13

corn
Core Sound Clams with Gold Tomato and Corn Broth, 85–86
Hot-Smoked Trout and Sour Corn Chowda, 77–78
yellow corn flour, 48

Country Fried Potatoes with Onions and Green Peppers, *xii*, 121, 130

crab
  crabbing along Neuse River, 41–42
  Deep-Fried Hard-Shell Blue Crabs, 51
  My Crab Cakes, 47–48
  seasonality, 27
  shelled, 26
  as shellfish, 23
  West Indies salad, 116
Crispy Brussels Sprouts with Garlic and
    Lemon, 125
Crispy Mullet with Roasted Jowls, Creamy
    Grits, and Fried Sage, 111–12
croaker
  cuts of, 25
  as finfish, 19
  seasonality, 27
  Shallow-Fried Bone-In Pan Fish, 49, 130
Croatan National Forest, 60
crowder peas: Skillet Succotash, 122–23
Cucumber, Onion, and Herb Salad, 126, 131
Culinary Institute of America (CIA), 5–6
curing seafood, 59–60. *See also* grilling,
    smoking, and charcoaling seafood
cuts of fish, 25, *25–26*

D

Daniel, Manhattan, 4–5
Deep-Fried Hard-Shell Blue Crabs, 51
deep-frying
  Deep-Fried Hard-Shell Blue Crabs, 51
  Fried Salt, Pepper, and Jalapeño Squid,
    53–54
  Fried Seafood Platter with Salsa Criolla
    (*Jalea*), 56–57
  Saltbox's Famous Shrimp Roll, 50
  Scallop Fritters, 52

dill: Monkfish Chowder with Sea Beans
    and Dill, 81
dogfish
  cuts of, 25
  Grilled Dogfish with Red Jalapeño Rub, 65
  as loin fish, 24
  seasonality, 27
Door to Dock, 14
dredge
  All-Purpose (AP) Seafood Dredge, 40
  calabash style, 48
dressed cut, 26
dumplings
  Grits Dumplings, 105
Durham, North Carolina, 8, *9*, 10–11, 13, *16*

E

Eastern North Carolina
  clambakes, 62
  cuts of fish, 25
  food traditions of, 1–3
  Freeman's Beach/Seabreeze, 46
  Native American heritage of, 60
  one-pot cooking, 75–76
Equinox (Washington, D.C.), 6
Escoffier, Auguste, 5

F

Fall Gathering menu, 131
fillet cut, 25
finfish, as fish variety, 19
Fish and Grits Sticks, 103–4
fish bones
  in stews, 75
  in stock, 30
  white bread bone cushion, 95

fish grease, storage of, 40
Fish Stock, 31
fish varieties
    cuts of, 25, *25–26*
    finfish, *19*
    flatfish, *22*
    loin fish, *24*
    menu development and, 14, 17
    round fish, *20–21*
    seasonality, 27
    shellfish, *23*
    shopping for, 18
    sources for, 28
flatfish, as fish variety, *22*
flounder
    cuts of, 25
    as flatfish, *22*
    seasonality, 27
Freeman's Beach/Seabreeze, 46
Friday's 1890 (New Bern, N.C.), 2, 113
Fried Cheddar Grits Cakes, 102, 131
"fried hard," definition of, 54
Fried Salt, Pepper, and Jalapeño Squid, 53–54
fried seafood
    about, 41–42
    Calabash style, 48
    Chicken-Fried Sugar Toads, 55
    Deep-Fried Hard-Shell Blue Crabs, 51
    Fried Salt, Pepper, and Jalapeño Squid,
        53–54
    Fried Seafood Platter with Salsa Criolla
        (*Jalea*), 56–57
    My Crab Cakes, 47–48
    Pan-Fried Oyster Dressing Cakes, 45–46
    Ritz Cracker–Crusted Bluefish Cakes,
        43–44
    Saltbox's Famous Shrimp Roll, 50

Scallop Fritters, 52
Shallow-Fried Bone-In Pan Fish, 49, 130
Fried Seafood Platter with Salsa Criolla
    (*Jalea*), 56–57
Frontera Grill (Chicago), 7

G
Galileo (Washington, D.C.), 6
garlic: Crispy Brussels Sprouts with Garlic
    and Lemon, 125
Glaze, Smoked Mullet with Cider-Sorghum
    Syrup, 70–71
Goodwin, Steve, 14, *15*, 85
gravy
    grits, shrimp, pork, and gravy, 100
    Oyster and Andouille Gravy over Grits,
        106–7
grease: fish grease versus other grease, 40
Green Beans, Long-Simmered, 120
Green Book Supper Club, 17
Green Peppers, Country Fried Potatoes with
    Onions and, 121, 130
Griddled Amberjack Collars with Fresh
    Thyme, 66
Grilled Dogfish with Red Jalapeño Rub, 65
Grilled or Broiled Oysters with Carolina
    Treet Butter, 64, 131
grilling, smoking, and charcoaling seafood
    about, 59–60
    Broiled Green-Tail Shrimp with Bay Leaf
        Butter, 61
    Broiled Panko-and-Herb-Crusted
        Triggerfish, 63
    Griddled Amberjack Collars with Fresh
        Thyme, 66
    Grilled Dogfish with Red Jalapeño Rub,
        65

Grilled or Broiled Oysters with Carolina
  Treet Butter, 64, 131
Hickory Charcoal Mullet with BBQ
  Butter, 68, 131
Salt-and-Pepper Charcoal Sea Scallops,
  69
Smoked Mullet with Cider-Sorghum
  Syrup Glaze, 70–71
Smoky Deviled Bluefish, 67
Whole Roasted Fish on the Bone with
  Salsa Verde, 72–73
grits
  about, 97–98, 110
  Basic Grits, 99
  Crispy Mullet with Roasted Jowls,
    Creamy Grits, and Fried Sage, 111–12
  Fish and Grits Sticks, 103–4
  Fried Cheddar Grits Cakes, 102, 131
  grits, shrimp, pork, and gravy, 100
  Grits Dumplings, 105
  Oyster and Andouille Gravy over Grits,
    106–7
  Shellfish and Grits Casserole, 108
  Shrimp and Grits Fritters, 101
  Skillet Speckled Trout with Warm
    Almond-Caper Vinaigrette and
    Cauliflower "Grits," 109–10
  Sweet Potato Grits, 100
grouper
  cuts of, 26
  as round fish, 20
  seasonality, 27

H

harvestfish. *See* butterfish
Hawaii, 4–5
Hector's (Chapel Hill, N.C.), 13

herbs
  Broiled Panko-and-Herb-Crusted
    Triggerfish, 63
  Cold Mustard-Herb Sauce, 38, 131
  Cucumber, Onion, and Herb Salad, 126,
    131
herring: Shallow-Fried Bone-In Pan Fish, 49
Hickory Charcoal Mullet with BBQ Butter,
  68, 131
hogfish (pigfish)
  as finfish, *19*
  seasonality, 27
  Shallow-Fried Bone-In Pan Fish, 49
hominy. *See* grits
Hot-Smoked Trout and Sour Corn Chowda,
  77–78
Hush-Honeys, 113–14, 118–19, 130, 131
Hushpuppies, 2, 48, 60, 113–14, 118

I

Iron Chef (television show), 6, 7, 98

J

jalapeño peppers
  Fried Salt, Pepper, and Jalapeño Squid,
    53–54
  Grilled Dogfish with Red Jalapeño Rub,
    65
Jim Crow era, 17, 46
"Joint" Seasoning, 33
joltfish. *See* porgy
jowls: Crispy Mullet with Roasted Jowls,
    Creamy Grits, and Fried Sage, 111–12

K

kitchen brigade system, 5
kitchen equipment, 28

L

Lemon, Crispy Brussels Sprouts with
    Garlic and, 125
Lemon Rice, 128–29, 131
Le Relais (Washington, D.C.), 6
Lespinasse (Washington, D.C.), 6
Le Tarbouche (Washington, D.C.), 6
Lewis, Edna, 7
Lindsay, Adrian, 17
lionfish
    as round fish, 20
    seasonality, 27
Locals Seafood, 13, 14, 27, 28
loin fish, as fish variety, 24
Long-Simmered Green Beans, 120

M

mackerel
    cuts of, 25
    as round fish, 20
    seasonality, 27
Melvin's Chicken Shack (New Bern, N.C.), 13
Miller, Amanda Wells, 14
mise en place, 29
Mobile, Alabama, 116
mollusks, shucked, 26
monkfish
    as loin fish, 24
    Monkfish Chowder with Sea Beans
      and Dill, 81
    seasonality, 27
Moore, Norma, 4–5, 6, 7, 8, 12, 13
Moore, Ricky, *xii*, 2, 4, 5, 7, 9, 12, 15
    culinary career, 4, 5–7
    culinary philosophy, 14, 17
    family background of, 1–3
    military life, 3–5, 98

mullet
    Crispy Mullet with Roasted Jowls,
      Creamy Grits, and Fried Sage, 111–12
    cuts of, 25
    Hickory Charcoal Mullet with BBQ
      Butter, 68, 131
    as round fish, 20
    seasonality, 27, 68
    Smoked Mullet with Cider-Sorghum
      Syrup Glaze, 70–71
Murray L. Nixon Fishery, 14, 28
mussels, shucked, 26
mustard: Cold Mustard-Herb Sauce, 38, 131
My Crab Cakes, 47–48

N

Native American traditions, 60
native fish, 14, 18, 82
NC Catch, 28
Neuse River, crabbing along, 41–42
New Bern, North Carolina, 1–3, 11, 13,
    41–42
Nixon, Ricky, 14
North Carolina dinner grits, 110
North Carolina Sea Grant, 27
North Carolina Wildlife Federation, 27
North Carolina Wildlife Resources
    Commission, 28
North River Camp Clambake, 91

O

Old Bay Seasoning, 116
one-pot cooking
    about, 75–76
    Cedar Island Fish Pie, 87–88
    Core Sound Clam and Sweet Potato
      Chowder, 79–80

Core Sound Clams with Gold Tomato
and Corn Broth, 85–86
Hot-Smoked Trout and Sour Corn
Chowda, 77–78
Monkfish Chowder with Sea Beans
and Dill, 81
North River Camp Clambake, 91
River Camp Fish Muddle, 89–90, 131
Singapore-Style Fish Collar Curry, 94–95
Stewed Clams and Country Sausage, 15,
92–93
"Warsh"-Pot Fish Stew, 83–84
onions
Country Fried Potatoes with Onions and
Green Peppers, 121, 130
Cucumber, Onion, and Herb Salad, 126,
131
Oven-Stewed Tomatoes, 124
oysters
Grilled or Broiled Oysters with Carolina
Treet Butter, 64, 131
Oyster and Andouille Gravy over Grits,
106–7
Pan-Fried Oyster Dressing Cakes, 45–46
seasonality, 27
as shellfish, 23
shucked, 26

P
Pamlico Sound, 60
Pan-Fried Oyster Dressing Cakes, 45–46
pan-frying
Chicken-Fried Sugar Toads, 55
My Crab Cakes, 47–48
Pan-Fried Oyster Dressing Cakes, 45–46
Ritz Cracker–Crusted Bluefish Cakes,
43–44

Shallow-Fried Bone-In Pan Fish, 49,
130
Parrot Cage (Chicago), 7
Peterson, Lin, 14
Picnic Season menu, 131
pigfish. See hogfish
porgy (joltfish)
as round fish, 20
seasonality, 27
pork
at church spreads, 127
Crispy Mullet with Roasted Jowls,
Creamy Grits, and Fried Sage, 111–12
grits, shrimp, pork, and gravy, 100
North Carolina pulled pork, 2, 11
Oyster and Andouille Gravy over Grits,
106–7
Stewed Clams and Country Sausage, 15,
92–93
in stews, 76, 92
Potatoes, Country Fried, with Onions
and Green Peppers, 121, 130
Provence (Washington, D.C.), 6
purple hull peas: Skillet Succotash,
122–23

R
Racial segregation, 17, 46
Rathskeller (Chapel Hill, N.C.), 13
Reynolds, William, 7
ribbonfish
as flatfish, 22
seasonality, 27
Rice, Lemon, 128–29, 131
Ritz Cracker–Crusted Bluefish Cakes,
43–44
River Camp Fish Muddle, 89–90, 131

rockfish (striped bass)
   as round fish, 20
   seasonality, 27
   washpot stew, 75–76
round fish, as fish variety, 20–21

S

sage: Crispy Mullet with Roasted Jowls,
   Creamy Grits, and Fried Sage, 111–12
Salad, Cucumber, Onion, and Herb Salad,
   126, 131
Salsa Criolla, Fried Seafood Platter with
   (*Jalea*), 56–57
Salsa Verde, Whole Roasted Fish on the
   Bone with, 72–73
Salt-and-Pepper Charcoal Sea Scallops, 69
Saltbox Bread and Butter Vegetable Slaw,
   115, 130, 131
Saltbox Seafood Joint
   catering truck, 10
   culinary philosophy, 14, 17
   development of, 10–11, 13
   Durham–Chapel Hill Boulevard location,
     13, 16
   inspiration for, 8
   menus for, 11, 14, 17, 130–31
   naming of, 82
   North Mangum Street location, 9
   Saltbox's Famous Shrimp Roll, 50
Salty Catch Seafood Company, 14, 28, 85
sauces
   Cocktail Sauce, 36, 130, 131
   Cold Mustard-Herb Sauce, 38, 131
   preparation of, 29–30
   Simple Hot Sauce, 39
   Tartar Sauce, 37, 130

sausage
   Oyster and Andouille Gravy over Grits,
     106–7
   Stewed Clams and Country Sausage, 15,
     92–93
scallops
   Salt-and-Pepper Charcoal Sea Scallops, 69
   Scallop Fritters, 52
   as shellfish, 23
   shucked, 26
Schweinfurt, Germany, 3–4
scoring, 95
sea beans
   Monkfish Chowder with Sea Beans
     and Dill, 81
Seabreeze/Freeman's Beach, 46
Seabreeze Fish Fry menu, 130
seafood, sourcing of, 14, 17. *See also* fish
   varieties
seafood bake, description of, 62
sea mullet (whiting)
   as finfish, 19
   seasonality, 27
   Shallow-Fried Bone-In Pan Fish, 49
seasonality, of fish varieties, 27
seasonings
   All-Purpose (AP) Seafood Dredge, 40
   "Joint" Seasoning, 33
   preparation of, 29–30
   Spice Boil Seasoning, 34
   Spiced Fish Rub, 35
sea trout. *See* trout
Shallow-Fried Bone-In Pan Fish, 49, 131
sheepshead
   as round fish, 21
   seasonality, 27

shelled crustaceans, 26

shellfish
as fish variety, 23
Shellfish and Grits Casserole, 108
Shellfish Stock, 32

shrimp
Broiled Green-Tail Shrimp with Bay
Leaf Butter, 61
grits, shrimp, pork, and gravy, 100
Saltbox's Famous Shrimp Roll, 50
seasonality, 27
shelled, 26
as shellfish, 23

Shrimp and Grits Fritters, 101

Shrimp Boat (Durham, N.C.), 13

shucked shellfish, 26

sides
about, 113–14
Country Fried Potatoes with Onions
and Green Peppers, 121, 130
Crispy Brussels Sprouts with Garlic and
Lemon, 125
Cucumber, Onion, and Herb Salad, 126,
131
Hush-Honeys, 113–14, 118–19, 131
Lemon Rice, 128–29, 131
Long-Simmered Green Beans, 120
Oven-Stewed Tomatoes, 124
Saltbox Bread and Butter Vegetable
Slaw, 115, 130, 131
Skillet-Fried Broccoli, 117, 130
Skillet Succotash, 122–23

Simple Hot Sauce, 39

Singapore, open-air hawkers' markets
in, 8, 10

Singapore-Style Fish Collar Curry, 94–95

Skillet-Fried Broccoli, 117, 130

Skillet Speckled Trout with Warm
Almond-Caper Vinaigrette and
Cauliflower "Grits," 109–10

Skillet Succotash, 122–23

Slaw, Saltbox Bread and Butter Vegetable,
115, 130, 131

Smith, Art, 7

smoked fish, 69

Smoked Mullet with Cider-Sorghum Syrup
Glaze, 70–71

smoking seafood, 59–60, 69. See also
grilling, smoking, and charcoaling
seafood

Smoky Deviled Bluefish, 67

snapper
cuts of, 25
as round fish, 21
seasonality, 27

soft-shell crab, seasonality, 27

SOP (standard operating procedure),
29–30, 114

sorghum: Smoked Mullet with Cider-
Sorghum Syrup Glaze, 70–71

soups. See also stocks
about, 75–76
Core Sound Clams with Gold Tomato
and Corn Broth, 85–86
River Camp Fish Muddle, 89–90, 131
Singapore-Style Fish Collar Curry,
94–95

Southwater Kitchen (Chicago), 7

speckled trout. See trout

Speckman, Ryan, 14

Spice Boil Seasoning, 34

Spiced Fish Rub, 35

spot
    cuts of, 25
    as finfish, *19*
    seasonality, 27
    Shallow-Fried Bone-In Pan Fish, 49, 130
Squid, Fried Salt, Pepper, and Jalapeño, 53–54
standard operating procedure (SOP),
    29–30, 114
steak cut, 25
Stewed Clams and Country Sausage, 15,
    92–93
stews
    about, 75–76
    Stewed Clams and Country Sausage,
      15, 92–93
    "Warsh"-Pot Fish Stew, 83–84
stocks
    Fish Stock, 31
    preparation of, 29–30
    Shellfish Stock, 32
striped bass. *See* rockfish
Succotash, Skillet, 122–23
sugar toad
    Chicken-Fried Sugar Toads, 55
    as finfish, *19*
    seasonality, 27
Sunburst Trout Farm, 28
sweet potatoes
    Core Sound Clam and Sweet Potato
      Chowder, 79–80
    Sweet Potato Grits, 100
swordfish
    cuts of, 25, 26
    as loin fish, 24
    seasonality, 27
Symon, Michael, 7

T
Tartar Sauce, 37, 130
"A Taste of Heritage" event, Hay Adams
    Hotel, Washington, D.C., 7
tomatoes
    Core Sound Clams with Gold Tomato
      and Corn Broth, 85–86
    Oven-Stewed Tomatoes, 124
trashfish, 82
Triggerfish, Broiled Panko-and-Herb-
    Crusted, 63
tripletail
    as round fish, *21*
    seasonality, 27
Trotter, Charlie, 6–7
trout (speckled trout)
    Fish and Grits Sticks, 103–4
    Hot-Smoked Trout and Sour Corn
      Chowda, 77–78
    as round fish, *21*
    seasonality, 27, 77
    Skillet Speckled Trout with Warm
      Almond-Caper Vinaigrette and
      Cauliflower "Grits," 109–10
Trust-Me Menu, 14, 17
tuna
    cuts of, 25
    as loin fish, 24
    seasonality, 27

U
uglyfish, 82

V
Vidalia (Washington, D.C.), 6

W

"Warsh"-Pot Fish Stew, 83–84
Washburne Culinary Institute, 7
Washington, D.C., 6, 7
washpot stew, 75–76
Westchester Country Club (Rye, N.Y.), 6
West Indies salad, 116, 131
white bread bone cushion, 95
white grunt, seasonality, 27
white/yellow perch
   as finfish, 19
   seasonality, 27

whiting. *See* sea mullet
whole cut, 25
Whole Roasted Fish on the Bone with
   Salsa Verde, 72–73
Winfrey, Oprah, 7

Y

yellow corn flour, 48
yellow perch. *See* white/yellow perch

Z

Zeppole, 114, 118